Praise for *The True Nature of Energy*

"Whether you are already highly intuitive or just beginning your journey into the investigation of the esoteric subject that is the energy around and within us, and how it affects our lives in so many ways, this book serves as a tremendous resource. Diane's thorough explanation of how we can harness the power that we all possess gives hope to us all in our journey to live a more empowered and fulfilling life. Combined with the excellent recommendations and very applicable strategies provided throughout the book, Diane guides us on an unparalleled expedition toward inner discovery and provides a masterful guide to tapping into our inner greatness!"

Victor Schueller, "Professor of Positivity and Possibility" www.VictorSchueller.com

"*The True Nature of Energy* has pertinent information about how our life energy affects all areas of life. Diane offers valuable information for us at this time of shift, offering an understanding of our intuitive nature and how we can develop it to understand our multidimensional experience here. Filled with tools and techniques for self awareness, the book offers us a practical way to see ourselves as energy. I highly recommend this as a way to understand yourself as an energetic force and direct yourself with dynamic exercises and information toward your greatest dreams."

Lyn Hicks, author, *The Lotus Project: The Art of Being a Woman*

"Philosophers—take heed! This is a book for people who are ready to stop being buffeted by the Winds of Fate and take ownership of creating their own realities. Unlike most 'applied metaphysical' handbooks, *The True Nature of Energy* provides clear, easy-to-follow instruction on how to fine tune and reconstruct the energies in our lives—towards a direction of our own choosing and design.

"Diane Wing parts the curtain on secret magickal techniques practiced by mystics and occultists and hidden from the uninitiated. This book provides clear and effective methods for us to tune into the energetic frequencies abundantly surrounding us and focus them towards manifesting what we truly want in our lives. No dogma required."

Maxine Ashcraft, process improvement expert

"A Book to Change Your Life—Reading this book has been such an eye opener in my life personally. It's a book of self-discovery and guidance, of personal growth and self-acceptance. I've been practicing the balancing exercises it provides to clear myself of emotion and to be able to see everything around me more clearly. With my trying to become pregnant, it's been amazing learning how to relax, let go, and focus on the positive energy surrounding me. I am finally able to turn a new page and begin the journey to my real destiny. With this book it doesn't matter what path you're on, what religion you follow, or what your belief system is. *The True Nature of Energy* deals with your energy, the energy around you, and how you can turn the negative energy into energy of supreme good."

Maria Briggs, Co-founder and editor of Fertilefairy.com,
editor of TheMammaHomemaker.com

"Clearly written and easy to understand. A tall order for a complex topic like this. Diane Wing's skills as a writer and energy worker are phenomenal. Highly recommended."

Lana McAra, bestselling, award-winning author
writing as Rosey Dow.

"I can thoroughly recommend this book as a guide to living. If Diane's way of seeing the world resonates with you, she will be able to help you to transform your life. Even if you want to argue with her explanation of why her techniques work, you will hugely benefit from implementing those techniques that make sense to you. In fact, reading the book in the process of editing it has changed me in positive ways. Her writing will do the same for you."

Bob Rich, Ph.D., Author of *Ascending Spiral*

THE TRUE NATURE OF ENERGY
TRANSFORMING ANXIETY INTO TRANQUILITY

DIANE WING, M.A.

FOREWORD BY CYNTHIA YODER

Library of Congress Cataloging-in-Publication Data

Wing, Diane, 1959-
  The true nature of energy : transforming anxiety into tranquility /
by Diane Wing, M.A. -- 1 [edition].
      pages cm. -- (Modern spirituality)
  Includes bibliographical references and index.
    ISBN 978-1-61599-196-9 (pbk. : alk. paper) -- ISBN 978-1-61599-
197-6 (hardcover : alk. paper) -- ISBN 978-1-61599-198-3 (ebook)
  1. Energy medicine. 2. Mind and body therapies. 3. Anxiety
disorders--Treatment. I. Title.
  RZ421.W56 2013
  615.8'528--dc23

Published by:
Marvelous Spirit Press, an imprint of
Loving Healing Press
5145 Pontiac Trail
Ann Arbor, MI 48105

www.MarvelousSpirit.com

Distributed by New Leaf Distributing, Ingram

Dedicated to those who choose to brighten the energetic pool.

Also by Diane Wing:

The True Nature of Tarot: Your Path to Personal Empowerment

Thorne Manor: And Other Bizarre Tales

Coven: The Scrolls of the Four Winds

Contents

List of Exercises

Foreword

The True Nature of Energy is an intelligent guide to the world as a vibratory place. Diane Wing walks you through your relationships, the places you visit and live in, your thought patterns and intentions, and the objects you collect and hold onto. Each of these arenas carries a vibration that may impact you. A thought carries a vibration that can bring your mood up, or send it crashing to the ground. An object from a hard period of your life may hold the imprint of that time and would be best let go of. Diane describes how these energies affect your mood and sense of being and how you can both protect yourself and improve your own energetic experience.

Diane draws on years of experience as a practitioner of Reiki and a coach to individuals who are energetically sensitive. She writes from a non-dual perspective, in which there is only one benevolent Source, and as she states, "every religion has its own name for this Source of Power." Thus, this book can speak to people from all walks and all traditions. The book is clear and articulate and offers numerous practices and visualizations to deal with the many situations you may encounter in life, such as toxic relationships, difficult group settings, or unsettled feelings that seem to come out of nowhere.

Anyone who feels impacted by the energies around them or wants to raise the bar of their own thought process and intention-setting should read this book. Her section on empathic people made me wish I had this book twenty years ago, when I began experiencing energies that I did not understand. She gives exercises for clearing and grounding your energy, which is so vital for energetically-sensitive individuals. Also included are energy shields and prayers to use in especially toxic situations.

One of the unique aspects of the book is the Wing Vibrational Scale that evaluates how your usual self-talk and habitual thoughts affect your overall vibration. I took this test and was surprised and informed by the results. The quiz is meant to be used over time as a tool for self-reflection and transformation. It is instructive to take honest stock of your habitual "set points"—where you commonly place your attention.

Another thing that sets her book apart is her treatment of the "shadow" side of emotion. She explores the transformative nature of the shadow and how to manage darker places when you experience them. Her treatment of the woods and the uplifting energies of the earth are enlightening and nourishing to read.

Diane also offers a holistic approach to raising your personal energy that includes caring for your body, eating a proper diet and exercising. There are many ways that you can get out of synch with your own inner rhythm and wisdom. Diane does not suggest any magic bullet cure. The "cure" is raising your vibration, one practice and one perspective at a time.

The best use of The True Nature of Energy would be to take it as a manual for self-transformation. Take two or three of the practices and adopt them for a length of time. Be your own observer and watch how your experience of life shifts. Or better yet, ask a friend to do it with you and compare notes.

To read *The True Nature of Energy* is to walk through the vibrations that make up your daily experience, while a gentle and wise voice guides you to observe, to change and to become more alive through the process. My copy is full of high-lighted sections and dog-eared pages. No doubt it will be a reference guide that I will return to often.

Cynthia Yoder
Author, *Divine Purpose: Find the Passion Within*
www.cynthiayoder.com

Preface

I did not always feel empowered. For many years I was puzzled by the fact that my optimism toward life in general did nothing to dissuade my feelings of inadequacy, disappointment, and lack of control. I intuitively sensed things around me, yet was often told that it was all in my head. It seemed as though others knew things that I did not. It felt as though my opinion did not matter. I did not know how to set boundaries and allowed my energy to be zapped by those who were overly dependent and took me for granted. I trusted the guidance of others more than my own sense of knowing what was best for me. I did not trust my intuitive knowing. I wasted energy on unhealthy relationships that lowered my self-esteem.

And then I woke up. I was tired of giving away my power. I realized that with each passing day I was missing opportunities to create the life I really wanted. I decided to take a chance and started making decisions that made me feel good, guided by my instincts, regardless of what others thought. The challenge was to overcome the fear, doubt, and worry that came with giving away my power to others. It was time to let go of behaviors and beliefs that held me hostage. It was then that I realized that everything was energy, everything held energy, and that the choices I was making served to enhance or diminish my own energy and the energy of relationships and situations.

I took back my power. I decided to get rid of anything that was taking away my energy. I made the most important decisions of my life and ended a confining marriage, changed jobs, and relinquished a long-held goal that no longer aligned with the ultimate vision of how I wanted to live my life. At that point, I began the journey of returning myself to my Self. As I shed the old way of being, I began to believe in myself, and the quality of my energy shifted to a higher vibrational level.

Each time an outmoded aspect of my life was removed, each time I refused to participate in the drama of others, each time I held my ground from a position of objectivity rather than emotionality, I freed myself from all that was obsolete in my life. As I cleared the lower level vibrations that had blinded me up until then, I began to trust my inner guidance and moved forward with calm certainty. My energy exponentially increased as I flowed with the intuitive guidance I received. The people and situations that held me back gently moved out of my life. Anything—people, activities, behaviors, beliefs, and perspectives—that vibrated at a lower level than mine held no appeal and new opportunities and realizations regularly came my way. The right job, the right relationship, and the right home became mine as a result. Shifts continue to come readily, and I flow with them, modifying my work, my relationships, and my beliefs accordingly.

My journey made me realize how many people are going through the misery and self-doubt that prevented me from achieving fulfillment for far too long. It is an uncomfortable place to be. You are ready to change your life, but are not sure where to begin. Everything seems like a struggle, and you are unable to clear the blocks that keep you stuck. *The True Nature of Energy: Transforming anxiety into tranquility* provides the knowledge, support, and guidance that make shifting so much easier.

I have created a life I love, waking each day looking forward to all the wonderful possibilities available to me! I vowed to inspire others to trust themselves to take control of their lives, and this book is the culmination of what I learned about energetic consciousness along the way. It exposes the secret of how to understand the energies within and around you, and how you can easily and intuitively tap into this abundant information. Becoming energetically aware validates what you are sensing and starts a personal evolution in the way you see yourself and the world.

The Universal Truth is that you create your reality, giving you ultimate responsibility for how you experience life. Everyone sees things from their own perspective, and that perspective has the ability to change with each new piece of information, the release of the old and outmoded, and the willingness to see things differently. Seeing through the lens of energetic awareness provides a means of removing all emotion, thereby allowing you to see yourself and others more objectively. You will enhance your awareness of how you open, close, and direct your energies with intention to be able to create the life you want. You will learn to sense the energies around you and use them to your advantage. This is the basis of true magick, tapping into the vibrations within and around you to achieve energetic consciousness and control. This is the key to fully taking charge of your life, building confidence through self-trust, and ultimately achieving self-mastery. When you master the Self, you are the master of your destiny.

To deeply connect with and sense the energy of Source is a powerful way to gain a profound understanding of our relationship with the Universe and of our creative power. Intention is the primary tool we use to shape our lives. In the words of one of my advanced energetics students, Annette Sadelson,

> "The essence of man is not shared with common words to Spirit. True intention is vibrational. I get it now. To connect with Spirit is not in grandiose or pious or even humble vocabulary, but with honest, sincere intent. That which we feel and the tonality of our voice decides or rather, moves our vibrational level up or down hence determining our mood and our ability to walk in Spirit, relax in chaos, or take a single step."

Centering on your overall vibrational level instead of one particular behavior gives you the power to simultaneously change all aspects of your life that need improving. The nature of the energy in your life either drives you toward positive activities that result in being motivated, inspired, and creative (high vibration) or moves you toward behaviors that diminish your energy such as smoking, overeating, or experiencing lack (low vibration). Changing the energies within and around you provides the power to change any condition in your life. By raising your overall vibration, you minimize or obliterate the lower vibrations.

This book is for those who are ready to take the next step in their personal evolution and want guidance through the obstacles blocking the path to self-trust. It is time to develop your inner guidance, to illuminate the patterns holding you back, and to become a clear channel of your own power.

Chapter 1 – The Nature of Energy

Energy is vast and pervasive. It is all around you, forcing you into a relationship with it. All interactions contain an energetic component. The unifying forces of the Universe are omnipresent in both living entities and inanimate objects. People, animals, situations, objects, and environments contain and give off energy. Energetic insight is a source of constant information, an intuitive knowing that increases self-confidence and removes the drama by seeing yourself, others, and situations objectively and accurately.

A Natural Ability

To encounter any of these things creates an energetic interaction. Everyone experiences these energetic exchanges, whether consciously or subconsciously. Because of this dynamic, it is possible to enhance understanding through insight into the energetic relationships that occur in the course of your daily routine and to perceive them objectively. What was once looked upon with emotion, fear, drama, doubt, worry, and guilt becomes pure when the underlying energetic pattern is revealed. As a result, decisions can be made and actions can be taken with a clear heart and mind. Enabling your natural ability to sense the vibrations that are constantly around you creates awareness of energetic shifts within the self and in circumstances outside the self.

Have you ever walked into a room and felt like you wanted to leave right away? Ever met a person for whom you had an instant dislike for no apparent reason? Been around certain people and suddenly feel exhausted? You have probably described a person or object as having "good or bad energy" or certain places as possessing "good or bad vibes." We regularly use phrases such as "that resonates with me" and terms like "harmonious." All of these references demonstrate that we are tuned in to the energy around us and attempt to describe what we innately feel.

It is a natural instinct, our inherent sixth sense possessed by every human and animal on the planet to varying degrees. The majority of people are aware of the energy around them, albeit on a superficial level. This is a means of intuitive knowing; it is the familiar sense of comfort or discomfort when you walk into a room that indicates whether positive or negative energy, or a blend of the two, is within that space. The vibrations could emanate from a certain person or group of people, from within you, or from a particular room or overall physical structure. Raising your energetic consciousness is to develop your natural intuitive ability and to open to a source of information that is constantly available to you. If you prefer the term *psychic*, it is simply the ability to perceive that which is beyond the five mundane senses of seeing, hearing, smelling, touching, and tasting. And just like some people have a stronger sense of smell or extraordinary hearing, so do some have a stronger sixth sense. While there are inherent individual limitations to the ability, just as with the other senses, it differs from the other five senses in that it is beyond physical limitation and can be developed and enhanced. Also, there are times when energetic sensitivity manifests itself in the other five senses, such as being able to see an auric field or hear the activity of imprinted energies from a time long past. With heightened energetic consciousness, resistance is lessened, flow is increased, and the ability to understand and use energy in specific ways is enhanced.

Energy has no limitations; it can reach anywhere it intends to go. With each gesture, thought, intention, action, and interaction, you move energy. You can choose to be sensitive to the wealth of information contained in the ether around you, or to remain closed off from and unacquainted with your surroundings. By understanding and being consciously aware of the energetic impacts you create, it is possible to improve relationships, to avoid mishaps, and to understand Divine Will while developing a singularly strong will of your own. It is riding the energetic wave in the direction the energy is naturally flowing, the essence of Divine Will, rather than fighting against the current so as to achieve in an effortless way, to manifest, and to thrive in abundance. It is a way to come into your power.

Awareness is the key to understanding the nature of energy. Awareness enables you to influence the way your personal energy flows and the way we project it out into the world. With the ability to sense the forces moving within and between you, it is possible to understand the underlying aspects of a situation. Heightened sensitivity to these forces expands your ability to understand your feelings and reactions, as well as those of others. It also enables you to tap into the vast abundance of Universal Energy.

By increasing your energetic awareness, it is possible to observe energy patterns and consciously change their texture. The ether that moves around and through all things, animate and inert, reacts to your thoughts, feelings, and actions. It connects all things. You make imprints in the ether with your words, actions, thoughts, beliefs, and emotions, and thereby affect the outcome of all events that follow. The way individuals choose to think and behave not only influences them personally, but also affects the vibration of the entire planet.

The techniques and energetic interactions discussed in this book offer alternative ways of perceiving the world and increasing awareness of the energy within and around you. There are numerous methods that vary by culture, tradition, and belief system to enhance your ability to move and influence energy. I encourage you to try not only those mentioned here, but to continue your explorations through other systems of thought and belief, ultimately knowing which are best through your own intuitive voice. To empower yourself fully and increase your effectiveness, I recommend taking aspects of all systems that speak to you, combining them, and adding your personal touch to the mix. It is important that your energetic awareness includes the types of techniques and beliefs that resonate most closely with your vibrational patterns.

Understand that with each shift, the techniques you employ and the beliefs you hold will change. Before embarking on this avenue of exploration into the self, make the decision to be open to a new way of seeing and sensing the world around you. Energetic consciousness allows you to ride the wave of vibrations and follow them to new opportunities. Flexibility is one of the most important aspects of energy, since change is inevitable and resistance to change creates discord within and around you.

Source Energy

When considering the nature of energy, it is essential to ponder its source. The essence of this energy is a conglomeration of everything that is known and unknown, every thought, feeling, and action, every aspect of every type of being. It embodies every archetype, every representation of gods, goddesses, saints, and angels, as well as the physical, emotional, mental, and spiritual expressions of all that is. It is the connecting force that binds us together and allows us to understand each other and to feel compassion for one another. If used to best advantage, Source energy fosters elegant interactions between plants and illness to affect a cure, between animals and their environments to foster harmonious relationships, between people to experience growth and enlightenment. When misunderstood or used to its detriment, pain, disharmony, anxiety, fear, doubt, and worry prevail.

The Source goes by many names: God, Infinite Spirit, The One, The Source of All That Is, and Universal Energy, to name a few. Every religion has its own name for this Source of Power. For now, suspend your preconceptions and religious notions of this energy and attempt to take a neutral position regarding its nature. Upholding the non-denominational quality of this text, we refer to this primary energy as *Source*. Source Energy has no gender, no malice, no love, and no impetus of its own. It connects all beings and things together so that each impacts the other. The attitude of the energy is neutral, having no attachment to outcomes, nor directing activity. Its nature changes as the beings that interact with it change. It holds vast amounts of information imprinted on it over time immeasurable.

Every person, creature, and plant on the planet makes the Source Energy's fabric ripple and change with each energetic impact and dynamic exchange. We can imprint upon it our hopes and dreams, hatred and anger, desires and goals. The way we are impacting this complex weave of energy is an awesome responsibility to be aware of; to understand that our choices affect what we manifest in each moment throughout our lives. We all tap into the same energy source. Each person chooses to brighten the pool with positive thoughts and actions or to pollute it with hatred and fear. We have the power to raise the vibration of the planet to increase harmony and peace or to diminish it into an unmatched state of war and hate.

Every being has its own energy field surrounding it, fueled by and connected to Source. By insuring your ultimate physical, emotional, mental, and spiritual health, you can generate a bright, positive energy. Sickness, poor diet, negative thoughts and emotions, substance abuse, and inactivity create a muddy auric field. Light or dark, your personal energy field affects every other on the planet, either bringing them to a higher level or depleting them.

There is a constant energy exchange between everything and everyone with which you associate. The awareness of these exchanges guides you towards or away from certain people, places, and actions. If you allow yourself to be energetically guided, it is a highly accurate compass steering you safely into shore and away from the dangerous rocks. Paying attention to the energetic interactions around you provides continuous learning opportunities by way of the information held within that exchange.

There are always factors and energies at work of which you are unaware. As a result, your actions are based on what you know and then can only surmise that it will have the desired effect. The Source has all of the information available to it that you do not, and so opening to the wisdom of Source is the best way to accomplish goals. This does not exclude you from taking action toward our goals, but it does give you support that do not necessarily factor in when considering the probability of desired outcomes.

With the occurrence of so many simultaneous interactions, probability is the only indicator of what will transpire next. Until you make a decision, formulate an idea, or create a shift in thinking, all potentials have equal probability of taking place. Until then, anything is possible. This is well illustrated from within quantum mechanics: a particle is only a probability until detected. The action we take may support our desires or work against them and, either way, while *something* may happen, it may not be what we anticipated.

Nothing is pre-ordained and the next action can change the potentiality of possible outcomes to follow. Taking action can contribute to a specific effect, but is not likely to be the only factor or cause of the particular effect. Hence, to produce a desired effect, riding the wave or rhythm of Source Energy is your best bet. You need to take responsibility for the choices you make; they are the expression of free will, and the more closely aligned you are to the natural rhythm of things, the higher the likelihood of taking potential outcomes and making them actual. Energy cannot be forced to do what you want in the timeframe in which you want it to manifest. The Source has its own sense of time, and energies culminate into desired results when all other associated energies to that purpose align with it.

The ability to harness the Source Energy is available to everyone. Tapping into Source, being fully aware of it, and establishing a constant flow and connection is the ultimate goal. By so doing, you are able to flow with Source, acting in accordance with your true nature, and with the Self intuitively aligned with Source. Achieving this level of awareness allows you to go with the flow rather than against the grain, thereby experiencing harmony and success. Aligning your personal energy with that of Source Energy is the core of health, well being, and the materialization of our desires. Going against it makes life feel like a constant struggle.

There is a never-ending redistribution of energetic possibilities due to the perpetual bombardment of thoughts, feelings, and actions upon Source Energy. Opening to these energetic shifts allows choices based on the most up-to-date energy patterns. Getting in synch with that which is around you, whether it emanates from people, places, objects, or ourselves, is to experience the wavelength of the situation and understand its true nature. The guidance system you use to make these choices must include an understanding of the energies within and around you. To discover how to observe, interpret, and direct this abundant energy is to harness the power at our fingertips. By understanding and being consciously aware of the energy within and around you is to remove the drama from your life, enhance your intuition, and manifest your desires.

Chapter 2 – Vibration

Energy is the foundational component of energetic consciousness. The amount and quality of energy you have within you is contingent on your diet and overall physical health, beliefs, emotions, and thoughts. The energy that is within you emanates in bands of energy outside of your physical body, known as your auric field. Starting closest to the body, the first band is reflective of your physical body, the second of your emotional body, the third of your mental body, and the fourth of your spirit body. The larger the aura, the more energy and power you possess. If the aura is close to the body, the energy is low and there is a heightened sense of vulnerability and fatigue. When this occurs, the various aspects of physical, emotional, mental, and spiritual health should be evaluated for how aspects of each are contributing to the low vibrational pattern.

The amount of energy you have indicates the quantity you have available to apply to your daily activities; the vibrational level indicates the quality of that energy. For example, an individual may have a lot of forceful energy, yet a low vibrational level that has the potential to harm themselves or others with that energy. An individual who has lots of energy and a high vibrational level will use that energy for the highest good and create an atmosphere of harmony.

Energetic Consciousness

Energetic vibration can be understood as the frequency at which the personal auric field vibrates. The quality of the energy you have at your disposal corresponds to the quality of your life and to the types of experiences you have. The higher the frequency, the more open and connected you are to Divine Source Energy and the higher your level of understanding, personal power, and purpose. The lower your frequency, the more discord you will experience in your life and the more negativity you will attract. Higher frequencies feel lighter; lower frequencies feel heavier.

Higher frequencies can be seen in the visible light spectrum. Purple, the color of the crown chakra (energy center at the top of the head), which is our link to Source energy, is at a higher vibration than red. Red is the color of the root chakra, which is located at the base of the spine, and serves to ground energy within the body and is associated with the denser, physical aspect of our being. Additionally, a higher frequency consists of waves that are short and closer together, while lower frequencies have longer wavelengths.

You have the ability to raise or lower your vibrational level and to recognize where you are vibrating. Why is it important to know where you are vibrating? Lower vibrational levels are more likely to lead to difficulty in your relationships and in your life in general. When your vibrational level increases, you will be less tolerant of discord in relationships and of dissonant environments, ultimately letting go of old, outmoded behaviors and associations and attracting positive energies, relationships, and circumstances. Your vibrational level is also felt by others, so if you have an important meeting or want to give your most desirable self to your family, it is important to adjust your vibrational level so that they can experience you in the best possible way.

When you are vibrating in the lower frequencies, you may engage in thoughts or activities that result in much less energy to accomplish your goals and take care of all your responsibilities. When you are energetically aware, you can determine when you are getting too low in energy and then intervene and elevate your vibration using intention. Being conscious of your frequency enables you to do a check-in with yourself and view the situation more objectively to make sure that your perception is accurate.

Perception affects vibrational level. For example, if you look around your home and notice it needs cleaning, you might perceive the task as a chore, something that is an inconvenience, resent having to do it, and complain about it the entire time. Or you can perceive the situation differently and tackle the responsibility with gratitude for having a home, for the physical ability to perform the task, and for the desire to live in a clean environment, thereby creating a higher-level vibration. Complaining weakens your energy field, thereby lowering your vibrational level and your overall energy along with it. Your motivation to complete the task diminishes. Notice that when you complain, your energy level dips. Notice how your energy feels agitated when you are around someone who constantly complains. There is no right or wrong, simply objective energetic associations and frequencies, and you have the power to choose every step of the way.

The Wing Vibrational Scale

Vibrational frequency manifests in your thoughts, beliefs, perspectives, and behaviors. Expanding your energetic consciousness is a powerful way to become self-aware. To make it easy to understand the outward manifestations of these vibrational levels, I have created a scale and associated quiz to increase your awareness of where you are vibrating at any given moment.

The Wing Vibrational Scale is my conceptualization of where certain behaviors, emotions, and perceptions express themselves on an energetic hierarchy. By putting my observations and experiences into this format, it provides a description of each level that can then be used as a common reference when discussing the way in which vibration expresses itself at different frequencies. Before publishing the scale here, a qualitative research study was conducted to see how the scale and resulting score aligned with the quiz taker's current perspective and life experience. Volunteers were asked to confirm that their score interpretation accurately described what was manifesting in their life. Additionally, they provided details as to which aspects of the level interpretations of their particular score reflected how they were feeling at the time of taking the quiz. During the study, the majority of folks (94%) reported that their score interpretation was accurate.

For most of those who indicated that it was off the mark, people closest to them confirmed the score's accuracy. This is an example of the difference between perceived self-image and internal true self. We attract what we are, which is reflected by the vibrational level, so to validate the score for yourself, look at your life to see what is being attracted and which patterns are being repeated.

The Wing Vibrational Scale describes energetic frequencies from Level 1 (lower, denser energies) to Level 10 (higher, lighter energies) and represents levels that are possible to attain in a lifetime. While there are energetic states beyond Level 10, these are what are possible to attain while in our physical body and in a state of consciousness on the physical plane.

In general, the levels at the lowest end of the scale versus the highest can be described as:

Extremes of the Wing Vibrational Scale

Level 1	Level 10
Isolation	Integration/Connection
Weak	Powerful
Barren	Abundant
Unaware	Fully Aware
Saturn(restriction)	Jupiter (expansion)
Heavy	Light
Non-functioning	Highly Functioning
Unconscious	Conscious
Anyone in a State of Mental and Emotional Emptiness	His Holiness the Dalai Lama

The Wing Vibrational Scale shows energetic densities as physical, spiritual, emotional, and mental frequencies. Two *selves* are inherent in every person: the projected image that is intentionally designed to create a specific reaction from others and the vibrational truth of the person. When someone is projecting a "trust me" kind of persona, yet you feel as though this person is something other than s/he is leading you to believe, what you are sensing is that individual's vibrational truth.

Some people have successfully integrated the two *selves* and come across with integrity, consistency, and sincerity. They are consistent with the way they behave, think, emote, and vibrate. Those who manipulate, lie to, or deceive themselves or others are more likely to maintain two separate selves. That is right; I said "themselves" or others. They say one thing and do another. They may deceive themselves into believing that their behavior and external persona translate into true energetic shifts. Over the years, I have encountered many people who state outright that they have achieved a very high vibrational level, yet they complain, harbor fear, doubt, and worry, and blame others for their problems. While they believe what they are telling themselves, their vibration can be perceived as denser and heavier or disorganized and agitated.

Feedback from a Wing Vibrational Scale Quiz taker (scored 7.05) expresses this well by saying, "Although I am bright and sunny [on the outside], fear and anxiety is underneath as I move through my learning. As much as I hate to admit it, your test is right! My situation at home is so fragile it is clearly where I come from. Lately, fear is in the picture, so even despite my desire to operate higher, energetically, I do feel that [the score interpretation is accurate]. It is good to be honest; self-doubt is about wondering how I could manage my big mission without [my spouse]. I clearly am either riding in his energies or my own belief is lacking. Either way your test is on the mark even though I would love to ride a higher vibe." This is a woman in transition and moving in the right direction. She is experiencing some discomfort as she tries on a few ways of being in order to see which one feels right. Coming into yourself and ultimately into your power is no easy task; there will be discomfort along the way.

Another woman shared her insights after receiving a score of 5:

> "After I completed your questionnaire and received the results from you, I am amazed at how stuck I really was and seeing it on paper helped me realize that I needed a shift in my energy pattern now. I have begun to work on it myself and feel much better."

That is the intention of the vibrational quiz: to open the way to increased awareness. That is where the shift—and the work—begins.

Exercise 2-1: Find your vibrational level

Before we proceed, let us start by getting a baseline at where you are vibrating right now. Take the quiz and see where you fall on the Wing Vibrational Scale. Then look up your Vibrational Level in the score interpretation section. The interpretations are focused on how these vibrations manifest themselves and how they are experienced within the context of everyday life. In this way, you will be able to see where you fall and how you can progress from where you are to elevate your personal vibration.

As you go through the items, answer them as you feel in the moment and avoid overanalyzing the questions. Go with your first instinct. Remember, these are energetic levels, not personality indicators. Energies change over time, and this will uncover where you are vibrating right now. There is an expected fluctuation in vibrational levels based on current emotion, circumstances, and perception. The key is to become aware of where you are functioning energetically at any given moment.

You may take the quiz directly in the book, use a separate piece of paper to record your answers and score it, copy the quiz and use it as a worksheet. It's much easier for you to take the quiz confidentially online and have the computer score it for you instantly at:
www.forestmagick.com/new/WingVibrationalScaleQuiz.php

Wing Vibrational Scale Quiz Worksheet

As you consider the following questions, circle the letter in the column to indicate whether you agree or disagree based on **your current state of mind regarding your life in general.**

Question	Agree	Dis-agree	Score
I feel lost in my life	A	D	
All I do is give others what they need	B	C	
Everyone is trying to undermine me	B	C	
I act with integrity or not at all	E	F	
I am able to move forward with calm certainty	D	A	
I am afraid of change	B	C	
I am comfortable being alone	E	F	
I am detached from outcomes	E	F	
I am dissatisfied at work	A	D	
I am grateful for all that is in my life	D	A	
I am in high service* to others	E	F	
I am lonely	F	E	
I am motivated to take action	D	A	
I am not motivated	A	D	
I am on a lifelong journey of spiritual unfoldment	E	F	
I am on a path of growth	D	A	
I am open to other people's perspectives	D	A	
I am surrounded by unhealthy relationships	A	D	
I am unhappy at home	A	D	
I am usually worried about one thing or another	B	C	
I can feel energies around me	D	A	
I can use natural cycles and energies to my advantage	D	A	

Question	Agree	Dis-agree	Score
I choose the paths I take	D	A	
I continue to evolve	D	A	
I depend on others to survive	F	E	
I do not feel safe in my relationships	F	E	
I do not know what I want out of life	A	D	
I do what I want when I want to do it	F	E	
I do not get what I need out of life	B	C	
I do not have a clear sense of who I am	B	C	
I drift from one thing to the next	A	D	
I enjoy applying what I learn to enrich my life	D	A	
I experience abundance on a regular basis	E	F	
I experience effortless change	D	A	
I feel a sense of connectedness to Divine Will/Universal Energy	E	F	
I feel blocked from moving forward in my life	B	C	
I feel disconnected from myself	F	E	
I feel disconnected from others	F	E	
I feel fulfilled	E	F	
I feel guilty when I say no	B	C	
I feel I have control over the direction my life takes	D	A	
I feel in control of my emotions	D	A	
I feel inspired	D	A	
I feel stuck in my life	B	C	
I feel the need to convince others I am right	A	D	
I feel unfulfilled	A	D	
I feel useless	A	D	
I frequently doubt myself	B	C	
I frequently experience creativity	D	A	

Question	Agree	Dis-agree	Score
I have attained inner peace	E	F	
I have come into my power	E	F	
I have difficulty controlling my emotions	B	C	
I have no close relationships	F	E	
I have no hope for the future	F	E	
I have the freedom to create the life I want	D	A	
I have willpower	D	A	
I keep looking for the one thing that will make everything better	A	D	
I live a life filled with joy	D	A	
I need to do whatever it takes to get what I want	F	E	
I need to put people in their place so they do what I tell them	F	E	
I often complain about my circumstances	A	D	
I often feel anxious	B	C	
I often feel depressed	B	C	
I say what I feel, even if it hurts others	F	E	
I spend most of my time alone	F	E	
I struggle with uncertainty	B	C	
I take time for myself	D	A	
I tend to react emotionally to situations	B	C	
I use drugs and/or alcohol to cope	F	E	
I use my own intuitive guidance	D	A	
Life has meaning	D	A	
Most of my relationships are difficult	A	D	
Nobody cares about me	B	C	
Nothing ever goes right for me	F	E	
Nothing will ever go right for me	F	E	
Others are always telling me what to do	B	C	

Question	Agree	Dis-agree	Score
The world is a gray, dull place	F	E	
There are times when I prefer to be alone	D	A	
There is no one solution to everything	C	B	
What I do is no one else's concern	F	E	
Life has no meaning or purpose	A	D	

* High service means using your gifts as a way to bring value to others rather than enable or be in servitude/cater to them.

Scoring Instructions:

Add up the columns using the following equivalencies:

A = 1; B = 2; C =3; D = 4; E = 5; F = 0

Divide your total by 365 and move the decimal point one digit to the right to get your score on the scale. Look up your score in the interpretation section staring on p. 17.

The score will most likely reflect a number that is between two levels, such as 5.74 or 6.83. The granularity is intentional. Scores are rarely solidly at one level or another, since your experiences may include aspects of both Levels 5 and 6, as in the case of 5.74 scoring at the higher range of Level 5, with more aspects of Level 6 present.

Be aware of any resistance that bubbles up as a result of reading the interpretation. One quiz taker commented: "This does not sound like me at all (scored 5.2)." Friends confirmed that the score was very accurate for this individual and that she is resistant to self-awareness and change. One quiz taker commented about her husband's score: "I think it described him pretty well (scored 6.7). He did not think so at first but when I reminded him about the 'story' he keeps dragging around about his [family] and how that keeps him stuck/attached to them, then he had to agree. He also has low self-esteem and self image." This is a great example of how checking-in with someone who knows you well can provide an objective understanding of your score.

Avoid placing judgment on your score; it is simply reflective of how you are experiencing your life at this moment. It is also the beginning of a deeper exploration into your beliefs and how they color your perceptions of yourself and the world around you. You can choose a different way of being any time you would like and begin working toward it now, next week, or next year. If you are comfortable with where you are, then so be it. If you are uncomfortable with how you are feeling, then you can decide to make changes, and we will talk about strategies to accomplish that.

Now look up your score below and see where you fall on the scale. Read both level interpretations that your score falls between and determine which aspects apply to you. You may be experiencing all or some of the indicators at your score level. One quiz taker scoring a 7.8 felt she expressed energies at Level 8 most of the time. Scoring between the two, there are probably times when she still feels worried about one thing or another, even though she is able to quickly get past it. She is probably also aware that there is no one solution to everything. While she is most likely expressing the energies of Level 8 most times, there are times when her doubts that may lower her vibrational level for a brief time. Be open to how your score and the vibrational level interpretations may be personally manifesting in your life.

Wing Vibrational Scale Level Interpretations

1 = Manifests as: Mental dysfunction—Most discordant, most negative, unaware, unable to see how actions affect their lives, lowest level of self-awareness [e.g., severe mental illness, drug addiction].

Experienced as: Having no relationships, is withdrawn and disconnected from self and others, lonely, despondent; engaging in activities to deaden the senses to what is going on around them.

2 = Manifests as: Moments of lucidity about self and circumstances, but choose to remain as they are. Have a very low level of self-awareness and very limited understanding of how actions affect their lives and the lives of others.

Experienced as: Unhealthy relationships; see the world as a gray, dull place; intense selfishness.

3 = Manifests as: Not caring about how their actions affect others. Functioning at the lowest level they can get away with, dependent upon others for survival, abusive, controlling, closed minded.

Experienced as: Dependent, belief that nothing can go right for them, have no self-control or self-discipline.

4 = Manifests as: Making minimal effort. Satisfied to do nothing and experience no growth. Restriction, rigidity, aversion to change.

Experienced as: Feeling lost, useless, and unfulfilled; drifting from one thing to the next; being unmotivated.

5 = Manifests as: Often complaining, having frequent negative thoughts, feeling resentment, regret, discord, entitlement; generally egocentric and/or judgmental.

Experienced as: Not knowing what they want in life; feeling that life has no meaning or purpose; looking for the "magic bullet" that will make everything better; attracting difficult relationships, toxic people and environments.

6 = Manifests as: Drama, guilt, jealousy, and envy.

Experienced as: Feeling blocked/stuck/stagnant; not knowing who they are; giving away power to others; feeling like a victim; getting lost in the drama; having low self-esteem; not getting what they need out of life; feeling guilty about doing things to take care of themselves.

7 = Manifests as: Worry and anxiety, attempting to change or thinking about doing so.

Experienced as: Often experiencing fear, doubt, and worry; struggling with uncertainty and self-doubt; feeling depressed and anxious; responding from a place of emotion; understanding that there is no one solution to everything; learning from mistakes; ability to shift perspective.

8 = Manifests as: Possessing self-control and self-discipline; increased understanding and self-awareness; can see people and situations objectively and clearly; have developed personal will to accomplish anything they set their mind to; achievement focused, able to take action, use intention, and set goals; self-confident.

Experienced as: Seeing the world as a bright, beautiful place; life has meaning; on a path of continuous growth and evolution/development; being in control; having the freedom to create the life they want; motivated to take action; open to other people's perspectives.

9 = Manifests as: Knowing their purpose; easily clearing old, outmoded behaviors; open to new experiences ; seeing clearly, having insight; knowing the value they bring to the world, feeling liberated, coming to quick realizations, possessing passion and objectivity.

Experienced as: Discerning the energies around them and using this to their advantage; effortless change; choosing the paths they take; feeling inspired; moving forward with calm certainty; cultivating wisdom by using their own intuitive guidance and applying knowledge; living a life filled with joy, creativity, and gratitude.

10 = Manifests as: Full integration of the subconscious with the conscious self and ultimately with the Higher Self; coming into their own power and using it wisely; being in a continuous state of gratitude.

Experienced as: Life has meaning, feeling fulfilled, flowing with change and Divine Will; reaching a place of inner peace; acceptance, detachment from outcomes, sense of complete connectedness to the Divine Will/Universal Energy/Higher Self, abundance, power, integration, high service to others, spiritual unfoldment, self-mastery.

* * *

At Level 10 of the Wing Vibrational Scale, the term "spiritual unfoldment" is used to describe one of the attributes of the highest level of vibrational attainment. To know your Self is the key to life and to all energetic operations. Unfoldment allows one to make the self known to the Self. Expanding beyond your former self reveals your true nature in ways that were formerly unknown to you.

The unfoldment process—and it is most definitely a process, not a magic bullet—is the action of extending yourself beyond your former state, learning in a manner that opens the mind, heart, and soul to new ways of thinking and being. To unfold, the process of shedding and removing old approaches to life is required in order to reveal the power inherent in your being.

Unfoldment is also the process of developing your spiritual side and your connection with the Divine. In this way, the self opens to the abundance of the Universal Energy and taps into the unlimited potential available to you. Unfoldment allows you to increase your understanding about yourself, your purpose, and the unique gifts you bring to the world. The act of unfoldment may occur gradually or take place in a flash of insight. Through revealing the core self and your relationship to the Divine, it is possible to tap into your intuitive abilities and develop psychic awareness that has been blocked by outmoded ways of thinking. When unfoldment takes place, the will comes to the forefront, and you are able to step into your power.

Ultimately, the goal is to achieve self-mastery. This means control over thoughts and actions and the ability to ride the energetic wave to manifest desires. Control over your inner world influences what you manifest in the outer world. Cultivating willpower is essential to self-mastery, and then, ultimately, allows one to connect with the ever abundant Divine Will.

Elevating/Decreasing Your Vibrational Level

Now that you know the level where you are currently vibrating, you are able to shift it up or recognize what lowers the vibrational frequency. Awareness is only the first step; the next is to take intentional action. It is important to take control of your vibrational level and raise it up when you feel it slipping. Everything you believe, do, think, say, and feel has an energetic weight and impact on your life.

When your vibration increases, you no longer seek behaviors that cause energetic imbalances such as smoking, overeating, or other heavier vibrational weight activity. You will know it is heavier, because you will feel drained, anxious, depressed, and guilty. You will know when it is of a higher vibration, because you will have increased self-control and self-discipline. You will no longer tolerate energies that weigh you down and will see the world as full of potential. You will be fully on the path to growth and development and will feel propelled forward in new and wonderful ways.

States of being that raise your vibrational frequency are gratitude, self-awareness, self-confidence, and knowing your purpose. The attributes that lower vibrational frequency are fear, doubt, worry, negative emotions, guilt, and drama. How do drama, guilt, and fear lower your vibrational frequency? These carry denser energies with them, weighing you down. They attract more of the same, thereby restricting the type of relationships you have in your life. For example, when you find yourself attracting negative circumstances and relationships, check-in with yourself and realize what you may be saying or believing to attract these types of situations. It feels like you are carrying the world on your shoulders. These frequencies create chaotic and anxious energies. It looks like spikes or jagged random lines when seen with the intuitive eye.

Check how you feel in certain environments and around certain people. As your vibration rises, your awareness of those vibrating at a level below yours will be heightened. Old, outmoded relationships will fall away as a natural process of your evolution. Circumstances and people who are not aligned with the level where you are vibrating will go by the wayside. Your tolerance for discord will diminish. A job may be lost to open you to a new purpose and vocation. A longstanding relationship that has been a source of difficulty may end to open the way for healthier interactions. Lessons will come easier, and your understanding of why certain people and situations are in your life will crystallize.

With the knowledge you now have of the Wing Vibrational Scale, you can apply the levels to yourself and others, situations, objects, and places. When you feel energies around you, determine whether they are dense or light, restrictive or expansive, or aligned with your energy for your highest good or not. Do the energies in a situation prompt you to feel elated or guilty, stuck or purposeful? Place your intuitive reaction to the energies around you on the scale from 1 to 10. This helps maintain objectivity when deciding whether having it in your personal space is beneficial or detrimental.

Energetic densities and propensities revealed through the Wing Vibrational Quiz, astrology, tarot, Reiki, or any other tool or system of metaphysics are meant to show you where you are vibrationally and what needs to be addressed. These are not meant to predict your future or your personality; but is to show you the energies around you and ultimately within you. Once the details of these energies are identified, action can be taken to adjust, eliminate, and align vibrational frequencies to bring about the life you want to experience.

External Indicators of Internal Energies

In addition to the indicators at each vibrational level, you can use external indicators to better understand energies. We manifest externally that which is prominent within us, and there are several indicators you can check for hints of your internal life. The condition of your dwelling or personal space is a good place to start. If your environment is well taken care of and is clear of clutter, it is highly likely that you also take care of yourself and place value on your wellbeing. You probably tend to clear the outmoded on a regular basis and let go of negative thoughts and beliefs on a regular basis. On the other hand, if your personal space is disorganized, dirty, and rundown, you may want to explore what is keeping you stuck. Piles of papers and other items, closets full to the brim, and dirt hold energy in a way that keeps things stuck. This type of environment does not allow energy to gently move through the space, inserting rejuvenating energy and clearing it of unwanted vibrations. An immediate remedy to feeling oppressed is to clean up and clear out.

Take a look at the art in your space. Is it uplifting or dark and dreary? Does it point to the desire for solitude and nature or for crowds and excitement?

Take a look at the types of people you attract and how they handle their own lives. Are they living in a way that aligns with your core values and aspirations? Do they demonstrate kindness and caring or manipulative, self-serving behaviors? Are your relationships with them healthy or full of drama? Notice the patterns in your life; do you seek out drama? Do you choose relationships that are inspiring or disheartening?

Take notice of what you wear—the colors, the fabrics, the styling. Do you tend toward natural, lighter color fabrics or wear black or darker shades most of the time? Wearing black actually prevents the effects of negative bombardments when going to meetings or when you know you will be encountering people who make you feel agitated or exhausted. You are doing this subconsciously as a reaction to the perceived threat. Wear black over your solar plexus to block the energy.

Are your clothes mostly formal, business, or casual? Notice how you feel when wearing any of the options in your wardrobe. When you feel threatened or vulnerable, you probably tend toward darker colors; when you want to take on an air of authority, business attire most likely your first choice; when you wear casual clothing, is it when you want to feel relaxed and comfortable? Do certain outfits spark creativity? Each type of clothing choice carries with it a different energy. When you put on certain clothing, you are setting the energy for what you are about to do, as well as a reflection of the energy that is going on inside of you. I know someone who wears his grandfather's hat before sitting down to write. It puts him in the mood to create, allows him to feel the support of his grandpa, and has the energetic association of past writing sessions.

Pay attention to how your clothing reflects your inner feelings or how you want to feel. Purge your closet regularly and keep only those articles of clothing that make you feel great when you put them on.

Particular outfits can be a powerful way to deliberately shift your energy.

Internal Indicators of External Energies

Your body, your emotional state, and your intuitive reactions are excellent internal indicators of what is present in the energies around you. Use your body as an objective measure of your surroundings. Muscle tension, fatigue, stress or anxiety, weight gain, and shallow breathing are all indicators of energies that are not aligned with your highest good. It is important to separate bodily reactions that are due to actual, physical distress or illness and/or resulting from adverse reactions to medications. For example, people who suffer from *mitral valve prolapse* often misinterpret the symptoms of this disorder as panic attacks. A complete physical examination will help you become aware of any actual physical issues so that you can differentiate between those and your body's intuitive reactions.

Weight gain in particular is one way that the body tries to protect itself from perceived threats. If you have difficulty losing weight, ask yourself how safe you feel in your relationships, in your job, or in achieving your aspirations. What are you protecting yourself from? I know a woman who easily maintained a healthy weight until she was sexually assaulted, after which she gained 50 pounds. In exploring this phenomenon, she discovered that if she appears unattractive, then she will be safe from experiencing another attack. Her next step was to get professional assistance to address the mental and emotional distress created by the trauma and to take steps to feel safe in potentially threatening settings. Seeking to feel secure in your circumstances and elevating your self-esteem will go a long way in reaching a healthy weight and staying there. Rather than expanding your physical body for protection, it is possible to shield yourself by generating a larger, brighter personal energy field (aura).

Muscle tension is a clear red flag to energies that do not serve you. Determine where your body feels tight. Is it in your chest? Then the likelihood is that there is an emotional tie-in to whatever is going on in your relationships either at home or at work. Is it in your shoulders? This could point to feeling heavy responsibility for something, whether it is perceived or actual. Is it in your throat? As the communication center, tightness in this area reflects the lack of ability to be heard or to the lack of desire to speak out. This is often accompanied by shallow breathing. When stress increases, the higher up in the body we breathe; the greater the perceived threat, the more tension in the body. When this happens, consciously move your breath into your stomach. Breathe deeply and intentionally so that your stomach expands rather than your chest. This will calm the body, which will calm you emotionally, and allow for objective interpretation of the energies around you.

Good physical health boosts emotional and mental health. The diet you consume will have a direct impact on the amount of energy you are able to sense, accept, and channel. The denser vibrational foods include animal protein and fried, fatty foods. Higher vibrational foods include fruits, nuts, legumes, and vegetables. Your body's physical reaction leads to emotional reactions. Tension and fatigue can quickly turn into depression and worry, which can shift into doubt, fear, and low tolerance. These are all low-level energetic frequencies, which is why it is important to keep your body at the peak of physical functioning. The stronger your body, mind, and emotions, the more accurate your intuitive guidance will be.

Clearing and Grounding

As we walk through our day and experience life, we collect the energies of others onto our aura, which can make us feel heavy and tired. Grounding is a means of attaching your energy to the Universe and to the Earth, allowing you to feel stable, balanced, and protected. By creating a connection, both above and below, a conduit is formed to allow a steady stream of energy to flow through you. In this way, positive energy flows in from the heavens and negativity flows into the ground. To attach to both is to know an intimate relationship with Source, while experiencing an extraordinary relationship with the planet.

Clearing and grounding helps us rid ourselves of toxic energies and feel safe as we open ourselves to experience the energies around us. Clearing your energy is also important so that intuitive messages can come through without judgment based in fear, doubt, and worry. Denser vibrations serve to block intuition. Regular clearing of your auric field is essential to removing any obstacles to the information received from Source and from the energies you encounter throughout the day. This enables objective understanding and decisions based on the information that comes through.

A general rule of thumb is to ground and protect before starting your day, and then clear and rejuvenate after the day is over. You become a powerful channel of information when the vessel or pipeline is clear of blocks and energetic obstacles. You can employ several techniques to accomplish this sense of strength based on particular circumstances.

Grounding and energetically protecting yourself before heading out for the day ensures a calmer overall experience, with less impact from external energies. Initially set aside 10 to 15 minutes in the morning to do the following exercise. With practice, you will be able to do it in half the time. You can perform this technique inside or outside.

Start by closing your eyes and imagining tubes descending from the bottom of your feet and moving downward through the floor, the ground, the layers of the earth, and into its core of molten orange light. Begin to pull the orange light into the tubes and up through the layers of the earth, the ground, the floor, and into the bottoms of your feet. Continue to pull the bright orange light up through your legs, into your torso, and up into your head. Feel the bright orange light filling your body and the strength it brings. Take as much as you need. You are tapped into an unlimited resource when you are plugged into the earth's center. When you feel filled to capacity, stop pulling the orange light, but do not disconnect from the earth. This will help you to maintain a firmly planted feeling as you move throughout the day. You are now grounded from below.

Next is to protect from above. Picture a large column of bright white light coming down from the heavens and pouring down around your entire body. Imagine being coated in this light from your head to your feet. Envision the light as a solid around your body. Make sure all parts of you are covered. Now encase the white light with a thin, solid border of bright blue light. Beam the light out as far as you can. Choose targets for the light to hit, such as trees on either side and in front and back of you. If indoors, beam your light from wall to wall, side to side, front to back. Focus on making it brighter and wider. Now you are completely grounded and protected.

With practice, you will be able to perform this grounding method faster and more effectively. Try beaming the white light farther out each time, until you are able to touch objects several feet away all around you. If done correctly, you will feel energized, calm, stable, and ready to face whatever the day may bring.

It is not always necessary to connect in both directions. High-intensity situations require that you ground mainly to the earth; to do so stabilizes emotions and evens out extreme bursts of energy. There are times when immediate action is required to balance and stabilize sudden energetic upheaval. When there are sudden bursts of discordant energy, like anger or devastation, it takes you off center, creating vibrational irregularity, and makes us feel shaky. When you become upset or angry, your energy rushes to the upper part of the body, lighting up the areas that house the mental and emotional centers; the lower half, where you root and stabilize yourself, your hips, legs, and feet, seem nonexistent. Think about the last time you were in a situation that made you mad or took you into a state of anxiety. Were you able to feel the lower half of your body? Probably not. Under these circumstances, it is important to instantly ground yourself so as to avoid escalating the situation and to regain conscious control of your thoughts and emotions. Recognize that this is happening and simply make a conscious effort to feel your feet on the floor. Breathe deeply and feel yourself beginning to calm down. This method is also effective when feeling anxious or threatened. It allows the body's energy to root itself firmly in the ground and provides a stabilizing effect. This is an instant grounding technique that redistributes the energy and brings it gently down from your upper body so that you can breathe easier and clear your head, thereby allowing more effective responses and decision making. While the technique itself is simple, realizing that your energy has pushed itself upward is difficult in the heat of the moment. With practice, you will develop the ability to quickly discern the shift in your energy and respond by sensing the ground beneath your feet.

External energies are one source of harmonic dissonance within the personal energy field known as the aura. Our own thoughts and emotions are a source of discordant energies, as well. Keeping yourself clear of your own negative thoughts and emotions is essential to raising your vibrational level and to increasing the amount of energy available to you. By regularly clearing your energetic field and grounding, you will feel stronger and more tolerant of the energies around you. Clearing your energy serves to rid yourself of internal and external unwanted energies.

Dumping these energies after a long day will make you feel lighter and energized. I recommend going outside and standing on a patch of ground (not concrete) to perform this exercise. Close your eyes and take a few deep breaths. Start at your head and take all of the negative thoughts that swirl around, all the doubts about yourself and your life, and all of the self-deprecating statements you make on a regular basis. Accumulate them in a ball and allow them to drain from your head and down your neck. At the throat, take all of the things you wish you had said and all of the things you wish you had not said, and combine them with the negative thoughts. Let all of these flow into your chest where your emotions live, and let go of all the pain, hurt, and disappointment you have experienced in your relationships. These heavy energies are now mingled with the negativity from your head and throat. Move them together into your stomach, where they accumulate with the dense vibrations of stress and fear. Allow yourself to release these altogether and let them flow down your legs, out the bottoms of your feet, and into the ground. Allow all the stress of the day, your worry, doubt, and fear to drain from your body, starting at the head and moving all the way down your arms, your torso, your legs, and out the bottoms of your feet. Let the negative energy flow into the ground (Mother Earth will cleanse it) until there is nothing left.

When you feel empty, open your eyes. Look around you. After performing this dumping exercise, all of my clients report either a profound clarity of their physical vision, that the trees look closer and more vivid, or an intense lightness of being, like a huge weight has been lifted.

After dumping all of those dense vibrations, it is important to immediately and intentionally fill yourself with clean Earth energy to avoid random energies entering you. Move about ten feet from where you dumped the negativity and stand on a fresh patch of ground. Send your roots out from the bottoms of your feet into the core of the earth and pull up fresh energy, bright, orange light that flows up the roots and into your feet, up your legs, and torso. At your chest, mix the bright orange light with bright green energy for growth, health, and development. Envision is swirling in your chest, down your arms, and into your head. Feel the elation that this fresh energy contains and allow it to fill and rejuvenate you. Continue to allow this new energy to flow until you feel full.

Another method for clearing the energies of the day is to take a shower and use a sea salt scrub with lavender or take a hot bath with lavender sea salts. As you bathe, picture all frustrations, annoyances, and disappointments leaving you and pouring down the drain along with the dirty water. This method provides a good transition from the work day and into a calm evening with loved ones.

Performing clearing exercises at least several times a week is recommended. For times of unusually high stress, it may be appropriate to do one of these methods at the end of each day.

When feeling agitated, restless, or tense, or even to maintain your center, get out into nature. Natural environments clear and strengthen the aura and provide vibrant surroundings to enjoy. The type of natural environment is a personal choice. Many of my clients and students enjoy being around the ocean and letting the sound of crashing waves, the call of the seagulls, and the smell of the salt air cleanse and calm them. My favorite natural environment is the forest. The earthy fragrance, the scurrying of chipmunks and squirrels, and the seasonal changes of the trees make me feel peaceful and radiant. As I walk, I attach my auric field to the trees on either side of the path, allowing me to pull in fresh energy while dumping negative or stale energy into the earth through my feet. With each step, energy blocks are eliminated and replaced with the vital green energy of the trees. The woods encourage my chakras or energy centers to open wider to accept the life force of the trees. The volume of positive energy flowing into me pushes away negativity and allows the light to flourish within me.

Exercise 2-2: Find Your Ideal Energizing Environment

> It is important that you find the environment that resonates with your vibratory pattern. For some, it may be the ocean; for others, mountain, meadow, cave, or lake environments may provide the ultimate sanctuary. You will know that you have found it when you experience a strong sense of comfort, peace, and openness. Where do you feel most energized, calm, and open?

Chapter 3 – Energetic Exchanges

People have a huge impact on your energy and you have a similar influence on others. It is easy to be taken off center by what someone says and how they behave toward you if you are experiencing doubt and uncertainty about yourself or your situation. The vibrational level is a primary indicator of an individual's wellbeing. Being aware of your energies, the energies emanating from others, and how they affect you is critical to maintaining a high vibrational level. Every interaction is an energy exchange. Think about the people you interact with on a regular basis—your boss, your coworkers, your friends, your clients, your students, and/or your family. Their vibrational level can elevate or diminish yours.

Types of People

There is a variety of types of people in any environment. At work or in public places, you have no control over who is present in the space; in your personal space, most times you do have a choice. Evaluate the nature of the energy you tend to be around on a regular basis. The nature of the people in the environment can generate stimulating vibrations or toxic energies that can be overwhelming. Some of the low vibrational energies you may come across are those that criticize, yell, complain, or deceive. They may be energy vampires/drainers, slackers, gossips, complainers, liars, naysayers, practical jokers, or they may emit unreliable, needy, jealous, grumpy, controlling, or judgmental vibrations. All of these can be exhausting and draining if you let them be.

Exercise 3-1: Journaling About Environment

Ask yourself the following questions and write the thoughts and emotional reactions that come through.

- How do you feel in crowds?
- What is your most energizing environment?
- What is your most depleting environment?

Fear and Other Toxic Energies

The root of most toxic behaviors is fear of perceived threats. People react to what they are most afraid of and seek inappropriate or ineffective strategies to defend themselves against it. For example, a person who has low self-esteem may be jealous of everyone around her because she perceives them as better than herself. She displays demeaning behaviors toward others out of fear of inadequacy and the resulting sense of vulnerability that follows. Rather than having the courage to take action and enhance herself in the areas where she feels inadequate, she seeks to pull others down so that she can feel superior to them.

Speaking of fear, it is among your three biggest enemies, which are fear, doubt, and worry. It is time to understand what you fear most: losing a loved one, the future, change, failure, success, and/or taking action—all prevent you from believing in yourself; these are perceived threats as opposed to actual physical threats. You doubt that you can make a difference, you worry that you are not good enough or are not trying hard enough. These perspectives block the flow of energy and prevent you from taking action toward creating your ideal life. I can hear the thoughts flowing in your mind…what if I make the wrong choice? What if I fail? What if so-and-so gets mad at me? What if I succeed; nothing will ever be the same.

You can choose to stay in fear or move beyond it. Only you can make choices that are best for you. If you feel that what is most comfortable is staying in fear and continuing your life the way it is now, then that is a choice. If this is your decision, here is the ideal formula to maintain fear:

$$Fear = Worry + Doubt + Vulnerability - Courage$$

Fear starts with doubt and worry and then is heightened when you feel vulnerable. It can be difficult to push through the fear and take action, especially when you have decided that you lack the courage to do so.

When fear bubbles up, take a moment to get rid of the negativity in a healthy way, such as using the dumping technique or taking a peaceful walk in nature. It is important to stabilize your energy to feel safe while making necessary changes.

Exercise 3-2: Journaling About Fear

Make a list of what you fear. Write the first things that come into your mind, and then go a little deeper. What are your reactions when you are afraid? Correlate your behaviors to specific fears that you experience. Are these fears justified? Can you take a healthier approach in dealing with them? What can you do to address them? How can you look at them differently?

Recognizing toxic energies of these types of people is fairly straightforward. You can feel a palpable change in the in the air around you when they walk into your space; the energy in the area will become muddy, cramped, suffocating, and agitated. Your body will react to their presence. You will feel instantly tired, your body will tense up, your chest or throat will feel tight, and your jaw will clench. Notice the dip in your energy, a lowering of the vibrational frequency in the space. Take note of these changes and seek to avoid being in the presence of the individual if possible or limit the amount of time you spend with that person. You will notice a significant increase in the amount of energy you have once the association is curtailed.

In some cases, you do not have a choice as to the type of people in your immediate environment. When out in public, at home, or at work, you risk taking on unwanted energies from others. Some people send harmful energies directly to you with thoughts of ill will, jealousy, and hate. Since energy has no spatial limitations and these thoughts carry harmful energies, they can reach you without being in direct physical contact with the person sending them. Any long term exposure to these energies can result in certain symptoms that occur regularly and are consistently present when around certain people. These include headaches, confusion/difficulty concentrating, a run of "bad luck," heavy feeling, skin eruptions/breakouts, physical illness, sleep disturbance, feeling drained, depression/anxiety that comes for seemingly no reason, and physical or emotional pain.

My grandmother used to say that these symptoms indicated that the person was suffering from the *Evil Eye* or *Malocchio* in Italian, a circumstance brought about by someone feeling envious or hurtful toward them. This is a clear example the weight energy carries and of how intention can bring harm to another. Once she determined that this was the case, she did a blessing with prayer to remove the negative energy and then tested the level of negativity by dropping olive oil into a cup of water. If the reflected light diminished each of the three times she performed the blessing, the Evil Eye was removed and the person's symptoms diminished or stopped altogether. She was performing energy work to remove the negativity someone had intended toward another. In all the years I watched her do this, the results were consistent and people walked away feeling better.

Intervention is necessary when these symptoms appear, whether you take action yourself or seek the assistance of a professional energy worker. While they can be indicators of actual physical maladies, it is amazing how many times there is no medical explanation for these symptoms, and no medication that can help them. The longer you are subjected to low-level vibrations, the more likely you are to exhibit one or more of these symptoms. Unless you deal with these energies, you will feel blocked, your work may suffer, the power you project will diminish, and your credibility and opportunities will be minimized.

It is best to focus on strengthening your energy against these forces and defending yourself from unwanted and toxic energies.

Exercise 3-3: People & Energy

> Make a list of people in your life that fit the descriptions above, and then answer the following questions.
> - Which type are you most affected by?
> - How are you affected?
> - How often are you around them?
> - What can you do to minimize your time with them?

Fortifying and Protecting Your Energetic Body

In order to protect yourself, it is important to understand what weakens the energetic body. Those who are particularly vulnerable have certain attributes in common. People with a weak auric field tend to feel exposed due to the small aura or energy field surrounding the physical body. An average aura should extend at least 6 inches from the body. I have felt auras that were an inch or less; in every case, the person was feeling tired, diminished in their thinking capacity, and hypersensitive to the energies of other people. They wanted to stay away from most people as a result of this vulnerability. The larger your auric field, the more protected you are from the influences of unwanted energies and the less likely you will be to experience the symptoms listed above.

People who are sensitive to psychic disturbances (empaths) have a higher likelihood of being affected by negativity. They are an open channel and take on the energies of others like a sponge. Depending on the energies of those around them, they may feel mental, emotional, or physical stressors as a result to this exposure.

People with addictions (alcohol, drugs, gambling, etc.) vibrate at a very low level and so are susceptible to energies that match this low vibration. Typically, they are in environments that enhance the negativity and serve to maintain or diminish their energy level, leaving them open to be affected by the unhealthy energies around them, as well as attracting more of the same.

People with low self-esteem give away their power by following blindly; believing that others know what is best for them. The lack of confidence lowers the vibrational level and attracts those who want to control and manipulate others.

Individuals who are generally anxious or nervous tend to have holes in their auric field. It is a Swiss cheese effect that occurs when people are overly stressed or consistently pessimistic. When I move my hand over the aura of these types of people, there is warmth in one spot and then a few inches away there is no energy at all. This creates a sense of being on edge. When there are holes in the aura it is easier to be taken off-center, to be prone to emotional outbursts, as well to become as easily fatigued. The holes serve as a gateway for negativity and unwanted energies to enter the person's physical body and create illness or emotional difficulty.

Engaging in a constant stream of negative self-talk diminishes the auric field. Entering into self-deprecating internal conversations serves to lower self-esteem and creates a sense of helplessness and hopelessness that ultimately leads to depression. It cultivates a mindset of pessimism and reinforces the belief that nothing can go well or that things cannot change or even that there is a black cloud following you around. The feeling that the world is not safe and that there is nothing that can be done about it stems from a lack of perceived control. This is accompanied by a lack of self-trust and a feeling of powerlessness. All of this weakens the aura and pulls it closer to the physical body.

Those who often engage in conflict or who are in contentious relationships have a weakened auric field. It takes quite a bit of energy to deal with unhappy, toxic, and abusive people and relationships.

Suffering from illness or injury makes you vulnerable to negative energies, as does not taking care of your physical body with proper diet and exercise. Excess weight is the body's attempt to protect itself. While there can be other reasons for weight gain, notice if you tend to gain weight when you feel threatened over an extended period of time. This could be in a personal or work relationship or situation. When under excessive stress, when feeling uncertain about your emotional safety, or concerned about job security, weight gain is likely. Many people who have suffered sexual abuse or trauma are known to gain weight, thereby subconsciously protecting themselves from appearing attractive to potential violators.

When the physical body is weakened, attention is focused on the illness or injury and the body uses the majority of its energy to deal with the malady. It is difficult to focus on higher aspirations if the foundational vessel of our being, the body, is functioning at a low level.

Exercise 3-4: Self Assessment

Review the section above and write down which aura-weakening behaviors you are currently practicing or experiencing. What can you do right now to change your approach, your behaviors, or to limit exposure to diminishing energies?

The best defense against negativity, both internal and external, is a healthy body, a strong auric field, and self-mastery. Self-mastery includes self-control and self-discipline, having respect and value for oneself, and the willingness and fortitude to take action.

Self-mastery = will + clarity + focus + wisdom – fear

Building a strong auric field increases self-confidence and self-esteem, promotes self-trust, and makes it much harder for these energies to affect you. Regularly performing the grounding, clearing, and protection exercises discussed in the last chapter is a good start to fortify your personal energy field. Being mentally, emotionally, and physically healthy is essential to defend against negativity and unwanted energies. Let us discuss some additional protection and fortification strategies to accomplish health in all of these areas.

Shielding

Energetic shields are used to block unwanted energies. These are used in addition to the white-light-from-above exercise (that helps to expand your auric field) when you need an extra layer of protection. I use several methods of shielding, depending on the situation.

In circumstances where it is desirable to block the energy coming toward you, but there is still a need to communicate, use the *plate glass* shielding method. The moment you realize that the person is projecting negative or manipulative energy toward you, envision a large pane of glass in front of you that extends from the floor to a foot above your head and arm's length wide. Their energy will bounce off of the glass and not have the opportunity to attach to your auric field. The plate-glass method is useful during meetings—in this case you can plan ahead—or in the moment when you realize that there is some threatening energy present. That is when you can flash the glass up between you and the other person at a moment's notice. It is important to become adept at using this technique before you actually need it, so practice envisioning the big plate glass window in front of you until you can do it quickly and easily. That way, you will be prepared when the situation arises.

For more profound and complete protection, use the *steel shell* technique. This is ideal for when you want to close yourself off from the energies around you—when taking public transportation, when in the waiting room at a doctor's office, at a crowded venue, or when needing time to disconnect from those around you. It forms something like a cloak of invisibility around you, where your energy is not felt nor do you feel the energies around you. Imagine being completely surrounded and enclosed in a dark gray steel shell around your entire body. Picture the shell as a thick metal barrier against the world. Make it as thick as you need it to be. Put rivets in it for strength. In this shell, you can peacefully read a book, meditate, or simply take a break from the world around you.

Prayer/Angelic Protection

To shield using the power of prayer, select any prayer from any denomination, or write your own. You need not have any particular religious belief in place. Choose the prayer that speaks to you. Psalm 23 is a powerful protection when said with intention and full awareness of the word, such as this excerpt: "Even though I walk through the valley of the shadow of death, I fear no evil, for You are with me" (ESV, 2001). There are variations of this and they can be found all over the Internet or in any prayer book. Prayers that are said quickly and out of habit from repetition are ineffective. When said with conviction, they transform into energetic shields that assist you in feeling stronger throughout the day.

If you work with angel energy, you can call in this type of protection. The most protective of the archangels is Michael. With his fiery sword he provides protection against all harm. Ask that he walk with you throughout your day to stand by and guard against all anything you do not want in your life. Envision this powerful archangel and imagine him walking beside you whenever you feel threatened.

Self-Awareness / Self-Confidence / Will

Knowing yourself at a deep level is paramount to feeling stable and expanding your auric field. When you know your triggers, your deepest underlying beliefs, and your motivations, it is much harder for people to take you off center by what they say and do. It provides protection from criticism and manipulation. Your ability to make decisions for your highest good and the highest good of those around you increases, for you will feel stronger and more capable to do so. Becoming self-aware allows you to have more control, inner peace, and more resilience, to create the life you want. True self-awareness is about knowing your strengths and limitations, your unique gifts, and how your choices and behaviors impact your future life.

Developing your will, an inner strength that allows you to control your reactions, persisting in the face of adversity, and setting a goal or intention and achieving it fortifies your resolve and solidifies your auric field. Think of people you have encountered who demonstrate confidence and who feel secure with themselves. Now recall how you felt around them. Odds are you sensed an inner strength, a solid aura, and the ease with which they moved through the room. This comes with knowing who you are and what you want. It is the product of believing in yourself and removing self-doubt. Having self-awareness, self-confidence, and a personal will attracts others who have the same mindset.

If you have decided that you do want to overcome energy-diminishing fear and negativity, developing and using your personal will is the best way to proceed. Your will controls your thoughts, experiences, and actions. The formula to develop your will is:

Will = Mind control + Self-discipline + Fortitude

This means that you develop willpower through controlling those negative thoughts through the act of self-discipline and applying fortitude to maintain this action despite discomfort. The will determines your next move, choice, and thought. It is your ability to control your emotions and impulses. It is what allows you to achieve self-control and self-discipline. Will is exerted when you seek to pay attention and concentrate on something of your choosing. It is the mechanism by which you are able to accomplish your goals and to persist in the face of adversity. It gives the ability to assert yourself with confidence. The will is reduced by self-deprecation, self-condemnation, and impulsiveness. It is bolstered by decisiveness, clarity and confidence. Willpower is your best defense against habitual negativity. It serves you in the pursuit of your true self.

Avoid what I call the Chameleon Effect. I had a client who engaged in many social activities, work functions, and family gatherings. She told me that with each group of friends, colleagues, and family, she changed to become who they wanted her to be; she became whatever she needed to in order to cause the least amount of friction and the highest level of acceptance. When she went home, she felt exhausted and could not understand why. The reason was because she was not being her true self; she was expending huge amounts of energy trying to be someone for the sake of others rather than for herself. Not knowing who you are makes you act in accordance with what others want from you, not with what you really want. When you know who you are and accept yourself at a core level, you have much more energy to create the life you want. This creates a consistency in your outlook, regardless of the various roles you play at home or at work.

When you know who you are and what you want, the fear goes away. When you understand your gifts and that you have a karmic obligation to express them, the doubt is diminished. When you accept yourself and what you are here to do, the worry of others not accepting you is no longer an issue.

Recognizing who you are at a core level is essential for you to come fully into your power. To do so requires shedding outmoded ways of being, removing limiting beliefs, and determining what you want your life to look like. Then you are free to create a life that you really want instead of simply accepting circumstances that serve to bewilder and frustrate.

No one is perfect. Nor can one ever hope to be. What you can do is to become more truly who we are. We can strive to accept our limitations and to enhance our strengths. It is also possible to sculpt ourselves into an individual to be proud of, in accordance with our personal concept of success, and thereby being more satisfied with who we are. Forming an accurate picture of who we are is difficult. Identifying the personality is different from determining an identity. We may project an outgoing personality when being evaluated by the outside world, yet could have a preference for quiet contemplation. We may be a mixture of both. Yet who we are when there is no one and nothing judging us is the core of what we must strive to uncover and to develop... and to accept.

The struggle to understand ourselves is to a large degree an exercise in discovering who we are, where we fit in, and deciding if our identities are in line with societal expectations. Many times, we define ourselves according to who we think we should be or who society thinks we should be rather than what our nature dictates. The identity is mistakenly tied to an occupation, role, or the expectations of others. We formulate a false identity by assimilating or rejecting the belief systems around us based on their prominence in our environment.

Some people tie their personal identities directly to others: I am a wife/husband, a mother/father, or a son/daughter. In this way, the individual gives up control to another's identity and loses his or her personal power in the process. If I am an employee who ties his/her identity to his/her company and the position is eliminated, depression and loss of direction may ensue. If I am a wife and I get divorced, my identity as a wife goes with the ex-husband and my world is shattered, leaving me to rebuild my personal identity. It is dangerous to tie ourselves too closely to any identity that can be taken away by circumstance. Rather, we can empower ourselves by building our self-image based upon our individual gifts and personal goals. This strengthens our ability to achieve inner stability and to minimize fear and anxiety.

False identity can also be a function of our past, present, and future: the past being a result of role models, upbringing, individuation, and child development issues; the present being our jobs, our roles (wife, mother, etc.), the expectations of others, the ideal versus true self; and the future based on our dreams and goals. Determining what our individual gifts are and deciding on our personal goals is a challenge. Wading through the jungle of psychological theory, popular opinion, religious doctrines, nature versus nurture, societal norms, cultural issues, and parental upbringing can be confusing, conflicting, and time consuming.

In order to see yourself more clearly, it is important to broaden the views of the Self and to elevate satisfaction levels with who you truly are. Everyone has something to contribute to the world. Each of us has the potential to achieve comfort within ourselves. As you observe your Self, you will unveil aspects of your true nature, allowing you to reach new levels of understanding, and increase self-satisfaction and enjoyment.

Exercise 3-5: Who are you?

Think back to what you loved when you were 7 years old.
- What do you recall that corresponds to what you still want today?
- What is in your life that makes you feel uncomfortable and restricted?
- What activities or which people or groups of people make you feel alive, inspired, and flowing?
- What are the top three things you want for yourself (do not worry about the "how" just the "what")?

*See Appendix A to take a mini-quiz and learn about tools for self-awareness that match your personal style.

Calm Mind

Seek to calm your mind, through meditation or other practice, and shut out the energetic and mundane noise that surrounds you. This provides a mental vacation that helps to reduce anxiety. It is also the best way to get the answers that lie within and that are available through Divine guidance. We tend to actively seek answers. We read, we listen, we ask for advice; we contemplate, we consider, we try this or that. We hope that others have the answers; those who have already treaded on the path we are looking to experience must know the secrets. As you consider their journey, keep in mind that their motivations and goals may be different from yours, and that their experience is being filtered through a different set of circumstances and perspectives. While what is relayed by these sources can contribute to your understanding, it is worthwhile to include your own unique perspective.

It is important to gather information and to learn as much as possible about the subjects that can help us move forward or that we are interested in. There is much to gain from knowledge and application of what has been learned. The reality is: the answers and validation we seek are available within us!

Readily accepting input from outside ourselves is habitual. Now is the time to include your inner voice as a regular source of valid information. Trust that this voice comes from the most powerful source– the Universe (Source). It is available to everyone. The key is to trust the messages that come through and to be able to tap into the knowledge on a continuous basis.

The external voices that we are used to consulting drown out the more subtle voice of the Universe. At the same time, we shut down messages from Source by our internal self-talk. Make time to quiet the noise coming at you from all sides, within and without you, and listen in silence for the messages that are meant for you. Trust that the information is accurate by feeling it deep within your body and soul. It will feel aligned with what you know is "right" for you as an individual.

Begin by sitting in a quiet place. "Ask" for a message about something that you are grappling with, and listen for the answer. Have your journal nearby to record what you hear and test the validity of the messages you receive as they appear in your life. The more often you are able to confirm the accuracy of the information, the more likely you will be to trust the Universe and your ability to pull the messages that you need when you need them.

When attempting to meditate, use whichever technique (Transcendental Meditation, etc.) resonates with you. There are times when we are overwhelmed with thoughts that flood into mind during times dedicated to peaceful contemplation. It is challenging to ignore these automatic thoughts, especially with so much going on in day-to-day living.

For active minds, here is a technique that can help to focus your attention without replacing it with words like a mantra. Light a candle. Near the candle put an ash catcher with a stick or cone of your favorite incense positioned so that the smoke can be illuminated by the candle flame. Turn off the lights. If you like, put on some soothing instrumental music (no lyrics to limit distractions). Sit in a comfortable position in front of the candle and incense. Focus your attention on the smoke rising from the incense. Watch how the candle flame brightens one side of the smoke and leaves the other in shadow. Follow the curling smoke and notice the times when it flows in a straight line. Allow your mind to drift with the smoke and feel it release all non-essential thoughts in that moment. If an intruding thought enters your mind, simply refocus your attention on the smoke and allow the thought to fade away.

Divine Guidance is the clearest form of advice you can get, as long as it can be objectively heard and not tarnished by doubt and negative self talk. With persistence, over time you will be able to minimize these intrusions and celebrate the ability to clear the noise enough to hear the important messages waiting to come through. Getting clear is one aspect of this process; finding the right environment, mental state, and physical comfort that increase your chances of getting a message is equally as important. Differentiating a thought from an actual Divine message takes practice; it feels different and resonates more strongly and with less stress than a thought does.

Ultimately, seek to trust yourself, your guidance, and the Universe. In this way, your path will be uniquely yours and the experience will meet with less resistance and a greater degree of empowerment. Your mind will be calm more often, as you listen for the inner voice that guides you for your highest good.

Healthy Body

Eating right, maintaining a healthy weight, getting regular check-ups, and exercising are important in strengthening the energetic body. Fruits and vegetables have a lighter, higher vibration than animal protein. Seek out relationships and circumstances that make you feel safe, and eliminate those that do not, to reduce your stress level and avoid excess weight. The healthier your body, the more energy it can channel, and the more solid your aura will be. The body houses the soul, and we must function in the physical plane of existence; therefore, it is essential to take care of the house in which lives our true essence.

Positive Self-Talk/Optimism

Negative thoughts, beliefs, self-talk, and self-perception block your energy and hinder the ability to discover and release your Inner Magick. Stop the negative self-talk and the negative things that you tell others about yourself—"I am worthless," "Nothing I do turns out well," "I cannot change." In most cases, this tendency is habitual and occurs automatically, with little to no forethought. The words pour from your mouth or occupy your mind with such regularity that it is difficult to imagine them not being there at the ready.

What you say is what you pull into your life. Negativity is discouraging and clouds your idea of what is possible. This negativity short circuits your ambition, your passion, and your motivation.

Exercise 3-6: Negative Self-talk

Take stock of your thoughts, beliefs, will, choices/ decisions. Take note of how many times a day you think or say something negative about yourself or your life. Are they aligned with what you envision for yourself? Do they support how you want to move forward or what you want to feel? Challenge the negative thoughts with a positive one. For example, when the thought, "Nothing I do turns out well," creeps into your mind or falls from your lips, challenge it with something you have accomplished that you were proud of, such as, "That table I refinished looks really great. I brought it back to life." Counteract the negative self talk with a positive statement and a focus on what happened that went well or that you performed well.

One way to prevent the dense spiral of energy created by self-deprecation is to wear a rubber band around your wrist. Each time you catch yourself, snap the rubber band and mentally yell "stop!" and then say something kind to yourself. Each time you stop the flow of negativity, seek to make the duration between when it starts and when you stop it less and less. Then add the goal of reducing the number of times you engage in this type of negative self-talk overall. Form a new habit of saying positive statements about yourself. The more you practice, the easier and more naturally you will be able to do it.

It is easy to focus on the things you could have done better. In contrast, when you did well, you probably simply check it off the list and forget about it. To tell someone else that you did something positive would feel like boasting, so you refrain from tooting your own horn. Even if you choose not to say anything to others, at the minimum, start practicing giving yourself private kudos for your accomplishments, big and small. It is okay to pat yourself on the back! If you fear that you will get a big head as a result, acknowledging your strengths will not make you conceited, but rather help you see the value you bring to your life and the lives of others.

Use all of your experiences to gain wisdom. In this way, you can benefit from the journey regardless of the outcome.

Wisdom = knowledge + experience + application

Energetic Defenses for the Workplace

At work in particular, there are defense strategies you can use to manage the energies you encounter throughout the day. You spend most of your day at your job, and the energies there—in the environment and among people you encounter—can be negative. These can become toxic and affect how you feel about your job and yourself. The role you play in your environment, your overall temperament, and those around you all work together to make your work life great... or really miserable. The goal is to project as much power and solid energy as possible. Use the strategies above, and add in the following to give yourself the best advantage.

In meetings, pick your power spot in the room. See which seat you are drawn to and feel most solid in. Never sit with the entrance door behind you; make sure you can see who is coming into the room. Do not sit with the corner of the table pointing at you; it creates an *energy dagger* that diminishes the amount of energy you have available. Avoid sitting with a window behind you, unless there is a building across from your building. It is best to have a solid wall behind you for energetic support. Watch the interactions between co-workers and attempt to see the energy passing between them. What is the vibrational level of the interaction? Does the energy feel smooth or jagged?

Set boundaries; do not allow yourself to be bullied. Cooperate, but not to your detriment; do not think of yourself as lesser or subservient. Maintain ethics and integrity at all times; lying and other unethical behavior depletes auric strength. Stay healthy—get enough sleep, eat right, do not party too much, do not work too much. Find balance. Do not feed into the drama of the workplace; detach your energy from what is going on around you. Avoid or minimize time with those who tend to drain you.

Beam positive energy and light into your workspace. Fill every corner of your space with an intention of peace and harmony. Remember to use appropriate shielding techniques when necessary— white light, glass, or metal. Do the advanced grounding and protection method before leaving for work and the instant method (feeling your feet on the floor) as needed throughout the day. Maintain a calm mind in the face of stress—remember to breathe, use visualization, and focus on the task at hand, not the drama.

There are external defenses you can use in your workspace, as well. Put a black tourmaline in bowl of salt and place it at the corner of your desk on the side where people come toward you as they enter your workspace. This will absorb any negativity that the person comes in with and keep it from having an effect on you. Clear the tourmaline as often as you feel is necessary, depending on the level of negativity at work. Run it under cool water, put it on a sunny windowsill, or clear it with white light or sage. Use smoky quartz to absorb negative energy, for putting a barrier of protection around you, to ground you, and to balance yin-yang energies. This can be placed on a shelf in your workspace. Remember to clear it regularly. Since most fire regulations prohibit burning anything in the workplace, use spray sage instead. Squirt it at each corner of the space.

Exercise 3-7: Instant Energy Booster

> There will still be times when you feel depleted and need an instant boost of energy. Sit comfortably and imagine a ball of swirling red light at the base of your spine. Envision the red ball of light becoming brighter and more intense. Feel its warmth at the base of your spine (root chakra) and spreading down your legs. Make the ball spin faster. At the point of its greatest intensity, allow the ball to release a bright blast of energy up your spine and out the top of your head. Picture it pushing open all of your chakras, ridding you of the dense energies that are blocking them, and energizing your entire body. Allow this energy to serve you for as long as you would like.

By practicing these methods and being aware of the energy around you, you will feel stronger within yourself so that you can fend off negativity and create a positive existence for yourself and those around you.

The Importance of Putting Yourself First

Being conscious of the energies that you project into the world is essential for the kind of self-awareness that leads to self-mastery. This awareness allows you to identify where energies are originating and if they are something you are absorbing or something you are sending out. What you send out into the world is reflected back to you in the form of relationships, situations, and level of joy or stress. Having control over these energies gives you the ability to eliminate that which creates discord and allows you to create the life you want.

When it comes to people, the primary issue I see that creates stress, exhaustion, and overall low vibrational frequency is giving away your energy by

- Only giving; never receiving
- Selfless Devotion Syndrome
- Saying "yes" when you want to say "no"
- Toxic relationships
- Taking on the energy of others

You may have been taught to put the needs of others before our own. You have the ability to see things in others, you see their potential and want to help them achieve it, but you are doing all the work. They take your energy without accepting personal responsibility to achieve their potential. Now you are lost in their energy, exhausted, and taken for granted. It is never enough, and the more you give, the more they want.

Here is one woman's story that demonstrates this concept:

Once there was a woman that made sure everyone in her life had what they needed. She cooked and cleaned for her family, she made her boss look good at the office, and she was always there when her friends were in crisis. It felt good to be relied upon and to help those around her.

Her friends and family, and even those at work, went to her with their troubles and trusted her to "fix it" for them. She devoted a great deal of time making sure that no one felt the pain of their poor decisions, lack of time management, or irresponsibility. She was tired all the time and wished that she had a moment to herself to read a book or to go to the hairdresser and have some down time. But each time she tried to fit it in her schedule, there would be another situation to resolve for those around her.

When those she cared about continued to come to her with the same problems over and over, she wondered why they had not learned anything from the last few times the same issue had come up. She began to resent having to put her needs aside to help them out of the same jams as before and could not help but think that they could handle a lot of their needs for themselves. But they just kept coming to her with their problems. No amount of energy she invested seemed to be enough.

Her demeanor turned from helpful to angry. She was tired from running herself ragged. She felt unappreciated and taken for granted. It was time for things to change, but how could she withdraw the help she so readily provided in the past? She worried that those around her would be mad and would ultimately reject her. She did not know how to show them that she still cared, but that she needed to take care of herself, too.

She needed help to transition into a healthier relationship with herself and those around her. It was time to get off the energetic rollercoaster. She began to realize that no amount of energy she could give would be enough to satisfy them and that she was not the cause of their problems. Does this sound familiar? All of that energy going out, with none coming in. The Universe sets up natural cycles of giving and receiving, and when we move energy only in one direction, it becomes a drain and causes lower vibrational frequencies to enter.

Exercise 3-8: Ask Yourself

> Are you too tired to take care of yourself because you are so busy helping everyone else? Do you say yes when you really want to say no?

You are dedicated to helping others and making the world a better place. My guess is that you are inclined to do this in your business and personal life as well. Are you the one who takes care of everything for everybody? Whether you are a caretaker for an ailing relative or friend, the one doing it all yourself in your business, or the one who is constantly imposed upon at home or at work, there are times that you absolutely must put yourself first. It is possible to do it in a way that will give you what you need, while having the energy to take care of all of your responsibilities. Taking care of yourself first is essential if you want to help others. You can actually increase your energy when you set boundaries and release unhealthy attachments.

I know many people who focus on what others need and put those needs before their own—whether it is out of desire, obligation, or guilt. We learn and grow by interacting with others. Learning to recognize unhealthy relationships and how you may be contributing to them is an important way to successfully overcome the patterns that breed frustration. You teach people how to treat you, and if you behave as though it is fine for them to disrespect your time and your needs, then that will be the nature of your relationship. By setting boundaries and consciously deciding where you put your energies in the relationship, you display a sense of self-worth. When you treat yourself differently, the whole world treats you differently. As you practice new behaviors and practice energetically observing these interactions, you will attract individuals who are vibrating at a healthy frequency and increase your confidence in the way you are interacting with those around you.

Let us start by exonerating you from the past. Whatever happened before, it represented the best you knew how to do at the time. So here and now, we are dumping any guilt that stems from the thoughts around "I should not have done this," or "I could have done that." Let us also suspend any blame that we may be tempted to place on others. They are who they are. You have chosen a path of growth and experiencing new ways of being; they may or may not choose to do so.

It is not selfish to take care of yourself; it is like when you are on an airplane and the flight attendant tells you to put your mask on first and then take care of those around you…this is the same thing, only in everyday life. Being in high service to others is different from being in servitude to others. High service is helping people help themselves with the reward of seeing others succeed. Servitude is being in a constant state of self-sacrifice to the point of losing oneself. I call this…

Selfless Devotion Syndrome

See how many of these symptoms you may be experiencing.
- You are tired from doing everything for everyone else. You give to the point of personal sacrifice and exhaustion.
- You feel edgy, agitated, and easily upset.

- You feel guilty when saying no to someone who asks for your help, regardless of the personal hardship experienced by you. Upbringing, whether religious, family, or the result of other societal influences, have guided some people, perhaps you, to believe that if you are not giving, you are not a good person. As a result, you feel guilty and are labeled as "selfish," either by yourself or someone else.

- Taking care of yourself always gets pushed off to the side so that you can give others what they need. You worry that if you put yourself first, others will get mad at you or suffer as a result.

- The more you give, the more people want. You get taken for granted, attract needy people, and those around you assume you will just "do it."

- You worry that if you change, the people around you will fall away from your life.

There is a real risk of losing yourself in these selfless acts. You get to the point where you do not know who you are anymore; your identity is dependent upon what others need and want from you. Keep in mind that people who want to control and manipulate you do not have your best interest at heart. Identifying those who lower your energy is the first step in limiting their effect on your vibrational level.

Your time and energy is a gift to others. You are not obligated to do so, but rather act out of concern and care. Some truly need a great deal of assistance; others have a sense of entitlement that drains those around them. For the latter, you can give them the gift of self-sufficiency or keep them stuck by enabling them to continue seeking help and never learning their life lessons. Allow them to make their own choices, face the consequences of their actions, and take responsibility for what is in their lives. Detach from their drama and their problems in order to take back control of your own life.

Compassion has a high frequency level. It seems easier to give compassion to others than to give this same gift to yourself: Be compassionate with yourself as you would with those around you. To make this shift takes time, so be patient with yourself. Give yourself the same consideration as you would to others.

Take a hard look at the type of relationships you experience, including how you relate to yourself. Relationships are reflections of who we are. We attract what we are, as well as the situations that are the lessons we need to learn. Look at the quality of your relationships; how others treat you mirrors how you feel about yourself. The relationship could be reflecting your fear...of rejection, of saying the wrong thing, of being criticized, of not being liked, of hurting someone else's feelings, or of being judged. There is a tendency to want acceptance from outside rather than inside. These relationships are in your life to mirror your doubts and insecurities, so that you can overcome them. Use them as a tool to change your perspective and overcome fears and doubts.

The energies inherent in certain behaviors correspond to what manifests as a result. The vibrational level of each behavior will attract the same vibrational level outcome. When you demonstrate self-respect, you receive respect from others. By demonstrating rescuing and fixing types of behaviors toward others, you attract needy people. The act of setting boundaries results in less resentment and more energy.

You have probably met people who cannot stop drawing negative circumstances to themselves. They hold onto all the drama and negative emotions and believe that these counterproductive thoughts are simply part of who they are. Worse, they hang onto them in the mistaken belief that this is what's needed to improve their lives. People wanting vengeance for a genuine or perceived wrong done to them are like this. The hardships and the pain cling to them, impeding their progress and preventing them from opening to the light. It creates a barrier that does not allow the positive to enter into the mix, thereby throwing them off balance. The shell around them continuously attracts more negativity, reinforcing the shell that does not allow the person to release it. When enlightenment occurs, it counteracts negativity and enables people to rid themselves of the weight that holds them back.

It is not a good idea to attach your energy field to someone who is predominantly surrounded by negative energy. It is likely that your auric field will absorb the person's trouble and anxiety, thereby creating a feeling of anxiety within you. The energy of a situation or person may be so negative that it is best to separate yourself from it.

Exercise 3-9: Practice Sensing Energy

If you encounter someone who makes you tired when near you, be aware that this person may be draining your energy, being unable to generate their own and keep the energy flowing within them. When interacting with someone for the first time, notice how you feel—distrustful, energized, focused, drained, etc. Take note of the flow of energy between you. Is it coming out of you and deflected by the other person? Does it flow back and forth between you? Practice sensing the pattern and texture of the interaction. Is it smooth or jagged? Is it hot or cold? Is it in a straight flow between chakras or in a more intermittent pattern? Feelings of resentment, anger, sadness and regret carry with them a heaviness that gathers strength the longer they linger.

The Six Keys to Changing This Cycle of Negativity

1. Decide that you want things to be different—this is the first step toward change. Align your heart and your head. Just saying you want things to be different does not make it so; in your heart of hearts you have to really want things to change. Take back your power by deciding that things can and need to be different. Things can only be different when your perspective changes, you release old beliefs, and sometimes, it means releasing old relationships that no longer serve you. This is scary; you do not want to hurt anybody or make them feel rejected, but the way things are right now hurts you.

2. Set boundaries—say "no" when something does not fit into your schedule, do not have the energy for, or if it is something you really do not want to do. If you are saying yes all the time for the wrong reasons—because you want to be liked, because your ego enjoys the stroking, or because you are afraid to let people down—you are doing more harm than good. It is possible to say no without destroying relationships and your reputation. There is a greater chance of doing a half-hearted job by taking on too much and

overwhelming yourself. Diplomatically saying no reinforces that you value your time and priorities and are not willing to take away from the truly important things in your life. Let others know what they can and cannot do around you. Part of this strategy includes not allowing them to continue to complain about the same things day in and day out. Ask them, "So what do you plan to do about it?" or "How are you going to address the situation?" Also, set time boundaries by not allowing them to take up too much of your time. Use the strategy of letting the person know that you only have 5 minutes or whatever time you determine to limit how long they stay in your space. A little self-care is necessary if you want to stay sane and maintain a balanced life!

3. Take care of yourself physically, emotionally, mentally, and spiritually. By looking good and getting the right sleep, exercise, and nutrition, you will have higher energy and a positive outlook. By clearing resentment, anger, and frustration, you have room for joy, peace, and love. Releasing negative thoughts about yourself and others opens the way for positive, productive thinking about your goals and aspirations. Your vibrational level will elevate and those vibrating at a lower level will gently fall out of your life.

4. Understand the role you play in your relationships—the caregiver, the rescuer, the fixer, the enabler. Stop the rescuing/fixing behaviors. Understand you cannot "fix" the other person. Spiritually and karmically, you are over-stepping your boundaries and inserting yourself into someone else's path, denying the other person the opportunity to grow. Give people back responsibility for themselves—this lets them learn the lessons they need to get in this life, if they so choose. Enabling others to be continuously dependent on you is not healthy for you or for them. When you are emotionally attached to the situation, it is difficult to see how it affects you.

5. Balance your needs with the needs of those around you. A balanced approach is the key to getting what you need, while still taking care of those around you. Your ability to help is severely diminished if you are exhausted and resentful.

6. Look at the relationship as an energetic exchange, without the drama. This allows an objective perspective. By becoming a detached observer without the emotion, you can see what is really happening in the relationship. This allows you to grow and move forward. You will see that those you had continuously helped still seek out assistance—what they really need are opportunities to take responsibility for themselves. You will realize that nothing you do will ever be enough to satisfy them. You are neither the cause nor the solution to others' problems. Look at the person's issues differently. Has this person repeatedly asked you for help, yet never takes personal responsibility? How is the energy you are providing helping or harming?

You may run into resistance from those around you as you begin taking care of your needs rather than automatically giving them what they want. Let people know that going forward, you are changing your priorities and will be taking care of your needs. By having what you need, you can give others what they need without feeling angry or resentful. As you begin making these changes, know that you are going to feel uncomfortable, as if you were being selfish and uncaring. This is because any new habit, however good, at first feels strange and unnatural, while any old habit, even if harmful, feels natural and as if it was a part of you. To keep moving in the right direction, get support from others who are facing the same challenges of putting themselves first and saying no to the things they do not want to do. You can also get professional support in the form of workshops and coaching.

Breaking Through Destructive Patterns

The next challenge is to overcome destructive patterns. These occur when we view ourselves and subsequently portray ourselves as lesser than we actually are. An example is not being able to say how you truly feel because you lack a solid sense of your own worth. This comes out in other ways as well, as in repeating patterns of choosing the wrong partner, holding on to certain fears, and doubting your ability to make choices that move you forward in positive ways.

The goal is to overcome these patterns by identifying where they originate, how they manifest in your life, and by being able to say straight out what you think and feel. Developing this awareness and skill goes a long way to creating love and trust in relationships. It is also valuable to recognize when others are interacting with you in destructive ways.

So, how do you know when there is a destructive pattern at work in your life? You are intuitive. A powerful method of tapping into your intuition is to use your body reactions to validate what you get intuitively when something does not feel right. You will know that you are heading for a destructive pattern when your body feels tense and your breathing becomes shallow. Whenever you feel uncertain, check-in with yourself; ask if what you are about to do is for your highest good. How does it feel in your body? Does your stomach get tight? Throat close up? Muscles feel tense? Do you hold your breath?

I have also seen these as signs of resistance to change, so be aware of whether it indicates intuition or resistance.

Exercise 3-10: Identify Draining Relationships

> Once these patterns are revealed, it is time to take action. To identify which relationships are draining you, make a list of all people you spend time with on a regular basis.
>
> Go through the list and put a minus sign (-) next to the people who are predominantly negative and toxic.
>
> Put a plus sign (+) next to the people who are most often positive and nurturing.
>
> Then stop spending time with the people on the negative list! If you do not believe that is possible—for example, if you are surrounded by negative people at work—do your best to dramatically decrease the amount of time you spend with them.

Surround yourself with positive friends: those working on their boundaries as hard as you are who are not enmeshed in their fair share of toxic relationships and therefore become somewhat toxic themselves. Essentially, you are choosing to be around people who are uplifting and motivated and eliminating or curtailing the time spent with those who weigh you down. Carefully choose the relationships in which you invest your precious time and energy to ensure that you experience the highest vibrations possible.

Enough is Enough: Cutting the Cord on Toxic Relationships

Finally, cut the energetic cord with relationships from the past and present. The physical or time distance does not eliminate the energetic ties you have with people. If thoughts of a person still arouse unwanted emotion despite the fact that they have crossed over or have been out of your life for years, this is a good opportunity to have closure on the relationship. These types of energies continue to drain you years after they are over. You may also want to remove someone from your present life. Make sure they are not there to teach you a certain lesson. If that is the case and you remove them, another similar situation will come about until you understand the reason they are in your life.

There are two ways I recommend for cutting energetic cords. The first is the Figure 8 method. Get comfortable in a place where you will not be disturbed. Envision a large figure 8 on the floor. Imagine yourself sitting in one loop and see the person you are cutting away in the other loop. Tell the person how they have affected your life, what you feel about the relationship, and all that you have always wanted to say to him or her. Release all of the negativity you have felt over the years from every fiber of your being. Empty yourself of all resentment, hate, fear, anger, sadness, and disappointment. You no longer need to hold onto it. When you feel that you have presented everything in your heart and mind, thank the person for being in your life and for all the lessons you have learned from the association. Wish him or her well and release the relationship with gratitude and blessings. In loving farewell, watch the figure 8 separate into two self-contained loops as the person drifts gently away from you. Continue to watch as you separate farther and farther away, until the other person drifts off past the horizon and out of your line of sight.

If you find that the person stops partway to the horizon, ask yourself why that is. What still needs to be addressed between you? Think about this and schedule another time to try again when the answer becomes clear.

The other way to cut cords is to picture a beautiful sword with a curved blade. Put jewels on the handle if you like. Picture the person you are ready to release and the cords that tie the two of you together. Imagine slicing the cords with an upward motion. Watch them break and melt away. The areas that used to be attached heal immediately, with no indication that the cords were ever there. If you have a difficult time cutting the cords, then ask yourself what the remaining attachment is to that person or why you are choosing to hold onto emotions associated with that person. Once the issue is addressed, try again.

Energetic Overwhelm

I have encountered many people who feel completely overwhelmed by the energies around them, especially those energies resulting from interactions with others. These highly sensitive individuals are called *empaths*. Empaths are very open, very sensitive, and are capable of absorbing the energies of those around them. They feel the emotional pain of others as though it is their own. They feel depressed and anxious for no apparent reason. Many of them are on anti-anxiety and antidepressant medications, because they are unable to differentiate what is theirs from what others are feeling; they take on the negativity of others. Some pack on pounds to shield themselves from the barrage of energies.

Understanding where their energy field ends and another's begins, along with learning to set energetic boundaries, is critical to their wellbeing. Empaths have a tendency to be very giving, devoted, and compassionate. Many caregivers have these qualities; so do those who are co-dependent. Learning to give without actually taking on the emotions of others allows them to have more energy and live a happier, healthier life.

Exercise 3-11: Are You An Empath?

To determine whether or not you are an empath, ask yourself the following questions. Do you:
- Hear that you "overreact" and that you are "too sensitive"?
- Get easily overwhelmed?
- Feel you have to cut certain people out of your life?
- Consider yourself intuitive?
- Avoid crowds?
- Get accused of being an introvert?
- Get accused of being antisocial?
- Avoid violent movies /TV shows?
- Avoid conflict?
- Take on the moods of those around you?
- Feel the need to withdraw and have time alone?
- Feel the emotional and/or physical pain of others?

If you answered yes to most of these questions, then there is a high likelihood that you are an empath. As an empath, you may have been told that you are crazy for feeling the way you do, that there is something "wrong" with you, or that you are cold and aloof because you prefer to be alone. You probably tend to be a sounding board for others to dump on and get grumpy for "no reason." Some may go so far as to say that you are "scary," "odd," or "creepy," because you know things about how they are feeling that they may not have told anyone.

The good news is that you are none of these things; rather, you are special, able to discern the energies of others in deep and meaningful ways. As a result, you are likely misunderstood for your highly attuned senses. Much of your distress can be attributed to being overly aroused by external forces. The fact that you are a compassionate, energetic sponge makes you a magnet for those needing relief from their own angst. These people are the source of the emotions you feel that seemingly come out of the blue. You may be feeling perfectly fine, and then suddenly feel an overwhelming sense of sadness for apparently no reason, then notice that someone nearby is feeling similarly. It is their energy you are feeling, not something coming from within you.

The sense of being overwhelmed by noise or by too many people around you is another indicator of empathic ability. The sheer volume of energy that these create is too much and results in energetic overload. It is upsetting to be around conflict, violence, anger, or negativity. At the same time, you have a tendency to be moved by music, art, or a touching moment you see on television.

This heightened awareness of energies in the environment makes it difficult for you to be in certain places, like locations where trauma occurred. You can tell when someone is lying to you or if they have good intentions. Your ability may extend to feeling the physical pain or ailments of others. With all of these sensations continuously bombarding you, you feel the need to withdraw and to be alone to recover. If you do not allow yourself time away from the constant barrage, you may become ill or extremely fatigued.

Other people sense on some level that you are an open channel, and tend to open up to you, even if you do not want them to. People in line at the supermarket may tell you all of their problems, intuitively knowing that you will understand and not judge. They may feel as though you can take away their pain. While you probably want to help, the danger is that this type of interaction can be overwhelming; it is an energy dump of negativity onto you. It will drain you, if you allow it.

Empathic awareness can take several forms. Some people are physical empaths, able to feel the actual pain, illness, or stress from others. This is especially true when you do not know how to ground and walk around wide open to receive these energies. When I began my work as an intuitive consultant, I was unaware of grounding techniques. As I opened to receive information for my client, there were times when I felt a sudden sharp pain in my head. When I shared this, my client would confirm a susceptibility to migraine headaches. This would occur with people suffering from sinus pain, backache, and panic attacks. Some of these energies were so powerful that it took a little while to shake them. That is why I emphasize the importance of grounding. My techniques can be found in the section on Clearing and Grounding (pp. 24-28), and I encourage them to be practiced on a regular basis.

Some people are emotional empaths. They take on others' emotions, such as feeling their depression, anxiety, fear, or joy. Self-knowledge is critical to stay aware of what is actual "yours" versus the emotions belonging to someone else. Seek to understand what triggers you emotionally, so that you can differentiate in that moment whether you are reacting to something or whether it is coming from someplace or someone else. Places where conflict occurred are especially difficult for emotional empaths. They can feel the sadness, grief, and panic of those who had occupied that space. Care should be taken to avoid areas that are known to possess negativity, such as prisons, battlefields, and psychiatric hospitals.

A mental empath is able to pick up on the thoughts of others. When around those who harbor negative intent, the thoughts sensed by a mental empath can be highly detrimental. Being around those who have kind thoughts and intentions uplifts the vibrational frequency of an empath rather than diminishing it.

Finally, a spiritual empath feels the energies of those who have crossed over into the spirit realm. Some may be full blown mediums, others may feel the deceased emotionally, mentally, or physically rather than actively communicating with the spirit. The connection they feel to the deceased makes them hypersensitive in the case of haunted buildings or when comforting loved ones left behind. This type of work opens them to the energies of both the grieving loved ones and the deceased. It is not your pain, do not take it on. Getting special training in grief counseling would be beneficial in this case.

Pay attention to the way you feel these energies. If left unchecked, your ability may lead to using drugs to self-medicate (both prescription and illegal), and taking medications you do not need, such as those who sense anxiety and depression from others and misinterpret it as suffering from it themselves. Getting clear on what you are sensing avoids the inaccurate belief that you are unable to control your emotions. The grumpiness you feel from overstimulation can be managed by balancing your time with people and quality time spent alone, rather than going to an extreme and choosing to spend the majority of time away from people. Those who are continually open to the energies around them feel stressed out, upset, and overwhelmed, feeling drained from constantly feeling the energies of others, especially energetic vampires. The sensation of feeling "burned out" may also prevail when empathic ability goes unnoticed.

As an empath, you need to cultivate self-knowledge, learn to set boundaries with people, regularly clear the energies you are exposed to before they have a chance to accumulate, take time to heal, and get help reality checking from trusted friends as you learn to determine which energies are yours and which belong to others. Pay special attention to the Fortifying and protecting your energetic body section (pp. 33-44) and incorporate the exercises into your daily routine. They will strengthen you against negativity and increase your tolerance so that you can enjoy being around others without feeling fatigued and overwhelmed.

Some basic guidelines that will help you keep your vibrational level up are:

- Do not watch the news on TV—it serves to increase anxiety
- Avoid negative people, when possible
- Avoid negative places
- Take time to be alone and rejuvenate
- Find peaceful places that calm you (outdoors)
- Declutter and organize your personal space
- Have a creative outlet
- It is not your "stuff," so let it go!

Toxic relationships are incredibly difficult for most people, and especially for the empathic individual. If you allow them, toxic people can be like vampires—draining your energy—mentally, emotionally, and even financially. When you are with them, your mood turns sour and you simply do not feel good. After you have been with a toxic person, you feel the need to shower yourself in some positivity.

At the core of most toxic relationships is low self-esteem, on the part of both the enabler and the toxic person himself. Generally, toxic people are filled with fears: afraid that they are not good enough, of losing control, of exposing their inner desires and wants. Often they have been victims of toxic relationships themselves. When people feel bad about themselves, they view other people's successes as a poor reflection upon themselves. They resent other people getting ahead. So, when another person is putting 'pressure' on them to perform at a higher level, the toxic person will search for a way to take the pressure off, usually by belittling other peoples' dreams, successes, wins, and goals.

Your sense of self-worth and your capability, and ultimately your vibrational level, greatly diminish if you are around a toxic person for too long. It is imperative that you take steps to ensure you stop the harm of people who are poisonous to you. Unless you are unaffected by negativity, it is best to avoid toxic people at all costs. A toxic relationship is characterized by behaviors on the part of the toxic partner that are emotionally and, sometimes, physically damaging to their partner. While a healthy relationship contributes to our self-esteem and emotional energy, a toxic relationship damages self-esteem and drains energy.

A healthy relationship involves mutual caring, respect, and compassion, an interest in our partner's welfare and growth, and an ability to share control and decision-making. In short, it is a shared desire for each other's happiness. A healthy relationship feels safe, where we can be ourselves without fear, a place where we feel comfortable and secure. A toxic relationship, on the other hand, is not a safe place. A toxic relationship is characterized by insecurity, self-centeredness, dominance, and control. We risk our very being by staying in such a relationship.

I have met people in search of the magic bullet that will "fix" their toxic partner, family member, or friend, or, at the very least, they are looking for someone to sympathize with them and agree how bad their partner is. They want to suck others into the toxic vortex of negative energy. Your vibration will be very limited when you are in constant proximity to negative or toxic people.

Before you attempt to address your relationship with a toxic partner, make sure your self-esteem and self-confidence are good enough for you to know that you will be all right if either of you end the relationship.

There are times when people do not take action from fear of ending the relationship. If you want to improve your relationship with a toxic partner, you have to be willing to leave that relationship if nothing changes. If you are unwilling to do so, you have very limited power available to you. Nothing will change if your toxic partner believes that you will not leave. Detach from the outcome and you will experience the higher vibration of acceptance.

Exercise 3-12: Practice Rating Relationship Energies

> Sit with that for a moment. Envision a relationship that is important to you. Which of the above components are parts of your interaction? How does your body feel when you think about your relationship with that person? Do you smile or frown? Evaluate the nature of the relationship and its corresponding energies. Do you feel your vibrational level lift or decline? If there is a great deal of drama and guilt, it would be a Level 6 relationship. If you allow each other space and trust each other, it may be a Level 8 or higher. Rate the relationship on the Wing Vibrational Scale (pp. 9 - 20).

Having too many relationships to maintain can be draining and overwhelming. An empath can benefit from limiting the number of people pulling on their energy. The first thing to explore is the feeling of "have to." Remember, there are no "have tos" or "shoulds" in life. There are only "choose tos." We get to choose where we invest our time and energy—and that includes determining which relationships we want to maintain. "Have to" indicates that our motivation to maintain the relationships is based on fear. But to create greater success and a higher vibrational level, we want to make decisions that are motivated by joy and excitement, as well as by our purpose and goals.

The Four-Part Inner Guidance System

You have a *four-part inner guidance system* that tells you when you are making decisions in alignment with your highest good.

1. Start by checking-in with your body's reactions as we discussed earlier in this chapter.

2. Then check in with your emotions. Think about your options one by one. Do you feel excited, happy, or upset?

3. Check-in mentally. Does your mind go to all of the problems that may arise as a result of a particular choice or does it embrace all of the potential and possibilities that may present themselves?

4. Finally, check-in spiritually. "Ask" Source if this is the right direction or choice. Is it for your highest good? Go with the first impression that comes through. It may be a simple yes or no response. If nothing comes through, ask for a sign. The answer may come later in

the day or later in the week, but as long as you pose the question, you will get an answer.

Your empathic abilities are a gift for understanding others, to get warnings to avoid negative people and places, for identifying where others need healing, and to capture energetic information you can use intuitively. You may be primarily one type of empath, or you may have the ability to sense energies in more than one way. Keep track of your experiences to determine which ones you are most sensitive to. Take stock of how you react to these interactions.

Once you determine how you pick up on and react empathically to these energies, stay aware of the way you interact with others, so that you can give them what they need while taking care of your own needs. Take a look at the role you play in your relationships, set boundaries, and release unhealthy attachments that weigh down your vibrational level. Doing so will bring you closer to having the life and relationships that allow you to express the best of yourself. By increasing your self-trust and self-confidence and by creating profound changes in the way you view the world, you will be able to determine what you want (and what you do not want) in your life. When you put yourself first, you open the way for an energetically balanced life of mutual respect, caring, giving, and receiving. A lot of people need you; position yourself to be to be in high service to others.

Be Energetically Conscious of Service Providers You Choose

Whether or not you are empathic, being acutely aware of who you are interacting with when you seek service providers is essential for your wellbeing.

Think about all of the service providers you interact with: your massage therapist, doctor, nail technician, esthetician, Reiki practitioner, coach, psychotherapist, intuitive consultant, or dentist. What is their vibrational level? Their energetic level is inherent in everything they focus on or create. Ideally, they are vibrating at a higher frequency than you are.

Service providers whose primary role is to raise your energy by removing blocks and strengthening your energy field are ideally at a high vibrational level, so that you can benefit from the interaction. If not, it may serve to pull at your energy and lower your vibrational level. Do you feel energized or exhausted after an interaction with the service provider? Do they complain about personal issues during the session? Do they seem angry or joyful? Does their energy appeal to you and is it something you want to incorporate into your own energy field? Does the service environment feel peaceful and harmonious? Use these questions to evaluate all types of practitioners and see if their energy is right for you.

Let's look at Reiki as an example. The number of Reiki/energy practitioners has increased over the years, and now more than ever it is critical to find the one who resonates with your vibrational pattern and needs, whether it is for treatment or to learn the art of Reiki yourself. Consider the energy of the Reiki practitioner: does he or she seem healthy, focused, gentle, caring, and open? Remember that the practice of Reiki requires that the energy be channeled through the practitioner and into you. Ask yourself if you want that energy going through this person and entering your energy body. Of late, I have heard many stories of clients and students becoming ill after a Reiki session or class with certain practitioners, and then getting the excuse that it was because they were adjusting to the energy. This is not a normal or healthy reaction to a Reiki treatment. After a Reiki session, you should feel relaxed, energized, lighter, and have a heighted sense of wellbeing. If you feel sick after a session, do not continue with that practitioner.

In the case of an intuitive consultant (Tarot reader, medium, psychic, etc.), before getting a reading, consider how you feel in the presence of the reader. If you experience any discomfort whatsoever, do not proceed with the reading. A reading of any kind is an energy exchange, a mingling of energies between you and the reader. If you are uncomfortable with the reader's energy, a reading with this person may cause a disruption in your energy field. Also, if the reader claims that you have a curse, dark cloud, or negative being attached to you and wants a hefty price to remove it, end the session and leave. A reader who presents you with such expensive strategies is looking for additional income and is not advising you in your best interest. Finally, it is important for you to feel that the reader provide information to you in a caring manner that is for your highest good. Harsh delivery of sensitive information can be detrimental to your state of mind. It is best to come away from the reading with a sense of hope, understanding, and clarity.

When selecting a life coach, get a sense as to whether or not the practitioner has their own act together. Receiving coaching from someone who is struggling with the same issues as you is counterproductive. If you are looking to commiserate, seek out a friend in a similar position and save your money. If you are serious about learning how to overcome obstacles, achieve your goals, and understand yourself better, then find a practitioner with expertise in the areas you are seeking to improve. For example, if you are looking to improve your effectiveness in your career/professional life, find a practitioner with business experience who has dealt with career development/transition and who understands the corporate/office environment.

If you are a service provider yourself, make sure that your energy is clear, calm, and put forth with intention for the highest good of your client.

Exercise 3-13: Practice Sensing Energies

When entering a gathering of any kind, such as a meeting, a party, or a networking event, check-in with how you feel emotionally as you enter the room. Separate the way you were feeling prior to entering the room from how the actual energy of the gathering feels. For example, imagine you are worried about how you will come across to people at a networking function. Categorize this as pre-function jitters. Keep in mind that there may be only one or two people in the room who are good energetic matches, so go in knowing that the majority of attendees are not the ones you are meant to connect with. You are searching for the right match. So how do you increase the odds of finding that person?

Upon arrival, take a few deep breaths, ground yourself by feeling your feet on the floor, and then open to the actual energy and dynamics in the room. Do the interactions feel casual or formal? Does the overall energy feel heavy or light? Are you feeling happy to be there or does the energy in the space make worry rise up once again? As you enter the room, sense where you should sit or stand. Allow yourself to be drawn to a spot or a person that feels comfortable to you.

Stay grounded and open to experience what comes next. Feel the person's energy and objectively interpret if he or she is the right match for you. Assess the overall result to validate that your vibrational impressions were correct. Were you energetically accurate in your choice of people? Did you feel energized and excited or tired and discouraged when talking to this person? Is the interaction less stressful and more productive? Practice this technique to enhance your energetic impressions when attending events and you will increase your skill and accuracy.

Chapter 4 – Energetic Imprints

Energy itself is neutral, yet can be imprinted upon and directed by intent. Specific energies can be imprinted upon environments and objects. The focus of the intent can heal or harm, create or destroy. We encounter both positive and negative forces on a daily basis. These forces can have a beneficial effect or a detrimental one, depending upon the physical, emotional, and spiritual strength of the individual. The nature of the energy is a blend of light and dark, such as when the destruction of a way of being takes place and is replaced by fresh, new thought patterns and corresponding energy. Nothing is purely one thing or another; there is always the aspect of one within another, as exemplified in the yin yang symbol -white within black; black within white.

Controlling Your Energetic Footprint

People can feel the type of energy being projected from an individual, albeit on a subtle level. We have the ability to control the type of energy we create within and around us through our thoughts, intentions, and emotions. Strategies for recognizing and modifying the energy we create, as well as the energies we encounter, appear throughout this book.

The energetic footprint consists of energetic densities in the physical, spiritual, emotional, and mental aspects of the self. The denser your energy, the more intrusive your imprint will be, and the heavier your presence will feel to others. The goal is to create the lightest possible frequency so that you are vibrating as close as possible to Source energy. To understand the impact of your energetic footprint, keep track in your journal using the Wing Vibrational Scale level interpretations. Assign the level number that feels most closely matched to the entry in your journal (no need to take the quiz each time). Also, notice the way the mood of others changes, for better or worse, with your presence. Do this daily, or even several times per day, as situations change and so does your mood, hence modifying your vibratory level.

Take notice of the energetic footprints of others and how they affect those around them. When I worked in a corporate environment, we had meetings with a hundred or more people in attendance. Before the meeting started, I liked to look around the room and get a feel for the energies contributing to the environment and ultimately to the task at hand. There were always at least a few "dark spots" in the room. The reasons for a "dark" energetic footprint could be many—a personal issue or loss, anger at having to be at the meeting or about the topic, or even a tendency for deception. As long as the number of dark energy people was low compared to brighter energy people in the room, the overall energy stayed fairly high. It was when the heavier, denser energy people were the majority that the goal of the meeting was not reached or a project was derailed.

So how do people experience your energetic footprint? What can you do to enhance your vibrational frequency so that you are a welcomed energy in meetings and gatherings?

Let us begin with the physical layer of your being. Keeping your body strong and healthy is essential for positive energy to flow within you. It is also critical to maintain physical health so that you are emanating positive energy. A diseased body may be an indicator that it is out of synch with the Universal Energy. This is easier to prevent than to cure. Align yourself with the energies of the foods your body needs and avoid those that are detrimental. Notice the difference in the way your body feels when you eat poorly. Honor and love yourself, seeing health as a natural way of being. This raises your vibration, and your immune system will respond in kind. As you come into an energetic flow, you will be capable of handling and channeling much more energy when you are healthy. If you find yourself getting sick frequently, ask how the illness serves you, for example, allowing you time to lie in bed, get attention you may not otherwise receive, or is it an outward manifestation of how you look at your life? Most passionate, active, productive people are rarely ill.

Now for the emotional energetic layer. Your emotions have palpable vibrational density. When you are joyous, you feel like you could lift off of the ground; you feel the lightness of your being. When you are depressed, you can feel the heaviness of that emotion. Many emotions are triggered by thoughts, and so keeping your mental house clear of negativity is critical to lightening your energetic imprint. Notice that people prefer to be around people who make them feel good, while people who spew negativity are avoided.

As spiritual beings, we are always in a state of creation. Whatever you focus on is the energy you pull in and generate. If you are filled with negativity, you will attract more of it. If you are optimistic, you will attract positive things. Keep track of how often you complain to others. You are pulling down your own energy, as well as the energy of the other person. How often do you commiserate with unhappy people, falling into their black hole of despair? You are exacerbating their downward spiral and creating a negative vortex for yourself. When you focus on the hate you feel for someone or something, it creates discord, not only for yourself, but for anyone in your energetic space. Additionally, it contributes to the discord of the planet as a whole.

Think about people who write negative things on Facebook and spew it into cyberspace. Notice how it makes you feel. How often do you succumb to fear, doubt, and worry about your path and where it is taking you? Think of what you have already survived; what is left to be afraid of? Be grateful for every experience and do not judge the experience as good or bad—it just is, and the vibration of gratitude exponentially raises your energy. To increase your self-confidence, focus on the things you do well, take account of your strengths and bolster them. Do not worry about what you are unable to do; that is why every person has their own special gifts—we can help each other fill in gaps. Celebrate your accomplishments and know that more are waiting for you. This will increase your self-confidence.

We have emotional, physical, and spiritual reactions to external energies. Take note of how you feel when something happens. Check in with yourself to see if you can look at the situation in another way to create a different reaction and raise your vibrational frequency. Many times your body knows something before your mind does, so pay attention to what your body is doing and how it is feeling. For example, the frequency of a lie is dense and negative. For those vibrating at a higher level, the body may react to that type of behavior in the form of nausea. It knows that this type of action is contrary to the higher vibrational level and creates a sick feeling. Hence, a person vibrating at a higher level tends to avoid behaviors that create a situation where they feel a need to lie and feel much better by simply telling the truth.

Finally, you will react spiritually or intuitively to a situation, knowing deep within yourself that something is wrong or something is very right. There may be times when you want to logically counter what your intuition tells you, but fight that urge. Listen to your higher self and what it tells you.

Controlling your energetic footprint is crucial, for it impacts everything you encounter. Throughout the day, you are actively imprinting your energy on others through your moods, thoughts, and intentions, as well as on the Universal Energy—a source which others are tapping into and picking up on your "stuff." It comes through and can be felt in your work, for it is infused in documents you handle, things you write, and things you create.

Think of an artist or a chef. What kind of energetic imprint is left when creating a piece of art or culinary dish? The end product reflects the energy you put into it. If you work with love, the end product will be beautiful. If you work with food and cook with love, it will taste better. If you create with passion, the result is exceptional. Creativity is not so much about art as it is about bringing yourself forward and expressing your purpose and what is inside you. It is essentially giving birth to your Inner Magick. You imprint on your own auric field, and it has an energetically tangible effect. For example, when I scan the aura of someone with low self-esteem, it comes across as holes in the energy field.

Exercise 4-1: Sensing the Energetic Footprint of Others

> At work, at home, or any place where the same people are in the same places, compare the energetic imprints left by others. At work, walk around to each office or cubicle and see how each feels slightly different, lighter or denser. Try to pick up emotional imprints in the space—anger, joy, frustration. Take note of how one differs from another. At home, do the same thing, but focus on each person's bedroom or space where they spend the most time. For example, my office at home has very strong impressions of my energy, as it is where I sit and create every day. My husband's office in another part of the house has his distinct energies in it, and my energy cannot be felt.
>
> Now consider how others may experience your personal space. What can you do or change to make the most positive energetic impression? [See suggestions below.]

When you feel your energy shifting into unwanted vibrational patterns, remember that you have the ability to control the energy and raise the frequency. Your awareness of the shift is critical to being able to take quick action. It is your responsibility to keep your energy at the highest vibration possible. The higher each of us can move our vibrational pattern, the better for the energy of the planet as a whole. Clearing yourself and your space is an important part of this continuous adjustment by decluttering, energetic clearing, and dumping your personal negativity.

Music can go a long way in changing your energetic patterns. When you feel agitated, listen to something soothing and feel your energy align with the music. Be careful of listening to head banging, angry music when you are annoyed; it will serve to exacerbate your mood and make your energy jagged and dense. I met a woman at an expo who insisted that her anger was soothed by listening to heavy metal music; she said it was cathartic yet was puzzled as to why she could not shake the anger. The music was actually keeping her vibrational pattern aligned with the lower level energies of her overall negativity. [To see the profound effects of certain types of music on ice crystals, read *The Hidden Messages in Water* by Masuru Emoto.]

Finally, catch your thoughts and make sure that they are clear of negativity toward yourself and others. It is easy to go far down the road of fear, doubt, and worry. One negative thought leads to another, and suddenly you feel exhausted, your motivation is gone, your confidence is in the gutter, and your vibrational frequency has dropped two levels. It is essentially a detrimental game of "what if?" that has gotten out of control. To illustrate this, say you are learning a new skill and are facing some challenges. Your thoughts may go in the direction of "This is hard. I cannot do anything right." Followed by, "If I cannot do this, then I cannot do anything." Followed by, "I am such a loser. Nothing ever goes right for me." And on and on. You can feel the downward shift in energy, even just reading it.

This happens so automatically, that it is difficult to arrest the flow of negativity. One way is to feel your feet on the floor and use the rubber band thought-stopping technique when you realize you are engaged in negative thought patterns. Each time you realize it, snap the rubber band to curtail the flow before going down a mental spiral of negativity. The key here is to stop the flow of these debilitating thoughts before they become overwhelming. The goal is to shorten the number of statements you experience each time it happens. The less time you spend mired in self-deprecating thoughts, the more energy you will have to overcome them. Once the flow is choked off, replace it with positive statements such as, "Yes, this is challenging, but with effort, I know I can do it. I will try again on my own and ask for help if needed." That feels much better, right?

Objects and Energy

Objects hold energy. While the objects themselves are inert, the energy they absorb actively moves within them. They can be imprinted with the energy from the environment that surrounds them, from the people who own them, and from the situations that they are part of. Handmade art objects contain the energy of the artist who creates them. Mass-produced objects are handled by multitudes of people— from those who handle the raw materials to those responsible for packing and shipping the item to you—all touched it and imprinted it with their energies.

It is important to be aware of the types of energy held within the objects that you interact with. They can impact your mood, your circumstances, and your physical health. The type of influence an object will have is dependent upon the nature of the energy emanating from it.

As you interact with various objects, it is important to be aware of the types of energy held within them and the kind of energy you are transmitting into them. Objects can affect your mood, your circumstances, and your physical health. An object's influence is dependent upon the nature of the energy held within it and emanating from it.

You imprint on objects throughout the day, and those items carry your energy with them. When you give someone a gift that you made or that you feel attached to, you are actually giving them a piece of your energy. Your energy is then "with them" whenever they are around the object. At the same time, items you receive from others carry their energy, so be selective from whom you accept gifts.

Objects created with a specific intention in mind, such as talismans, have energy imprinted on them by the person who charged the object. Unless you are the person who imprinted the intention, be wary of the motivation and energies channeled by the person who did.

Objects are imprinted upon constantly. Your energy and that of others goes into the objects you encounter. You can feel the imprints on objects. Those who are most sensitive in this way are called psychometrists; they hold objects worn by an individual and are able to read the energies imprinted upon them. Do not let others try on or wear your jewelry, for their energy can imprint on it and shift the vibrational pattern.

Used Items

Do you enjoy shopping at flea markets, antique shops, and second-hand stores? Before you bring your newfound treasures into your house, be aware that objects hold energy. Jewelry, crystals, and furniture are examples of objects that can hold the energy of the person who owned it. Be aware of this when shopping for antiques or estate jewelry. When you hold the object, take note of how it makes you feel. Do you experience a sense of sadness or of joy? Does it make your hand tingle? Can you see it sitting in a particular place in your home? In this way, you can try to pick up the nature of the energy of the former owner or owners. Avoid bringing objects into your home that hold negativity and make you feel tired or sad.

Jewelry and clothing are items to be particularly careful of when buying them used. Wearing an item that contains an undesirable vibration can have a negative effect on your energy level. To test the desirability of a particular piece, briefly interact with it. For example, if you are considering buying a necklace at an estate sale, try it on. While it hangs around your neck, sense the heaviness of it. Do you feel slightly nauseous? Do you feel energized? Does your chest feel heavy and are you having difficulty breathing? Does it feel like it belongs to you? Keep near you only items that make you feel good, especially those that will be closest to your skin.

Religious items from houses of worship, as well as personal religious objects, such as rosary beads, hold the energies of those that prayed on them, releasing their fear, worry, and pain onto them. A client contacted me to do a house cleansing, because she felt some unwelcome energetic activity in her home. When I got there, I was greeted by walls and walls of antique Christ-on-the-cross and the wounded Jesus in his mother's arms. They decorated every room in the home and were even hung on both sides of the stairway leading to the second floor. The cleansing ritual calmed the space somewhat, but to clear the space completely required removal of the religious relics or, at minimum, a heavy duty cleansing of each of the items. Since her husband was a collector of these items, they did not plan to get rid of them, so they compromised and removed some and boxed them up. The activity lessened, but is still present, albeit at a lower level. When purchasing religious statuary or other items, buy them new and clear them before using them yourself. We will talk about energetic clearing a bit later.

Keepsakes

Memorabilia, that is, bits and pieces of objects that remind you of a particular time, place, or person, contain the energy of those memories. Most people have a stash of concert tickets, snow globes, pictures, jewelry, correspondence, and countless other representations of special or significant times in their lives. The energy that clings to these objects holds the memory of the event as clearly as you hold it in your mind. Even general objects around your home that may be attached to a certain period in your life continue to emanate energy from that time and relationship, such as those you bought or received as gifts during an unhappy marriage. The types of memories associated with these various personal objects influence the overall energy that flows within your home.

If you have a penchant for a particular item, yet get the feeling that its energy is disagreeable, you can attempt to cleanse the object. Many times it is possible to clear the unwanted vibrations from. Other times, the negativity may be heavily ingrained into the item and therefore difficult or impossible to remove. In this case, it is best to part with the object as soon as possible.

Clear Outmoded Vibrations

The types of memories associated with these various personal objects influence the overall energy that flows within your home. When trying to distance yourself from certain memories or people, remove the objects associated with them from your home. Complete disconnection from these energetic influences will be impossible as long as you retain the associated items.

Keep the energy in your home clear by discarding all things that are no longer pertinent to your growth. It is important to go through your possessions occasionally. Discard anything attached to a negative period in your life, including clothing and things belonging to or reminding you of people who hindered your development or who caused you emotional or physical distress. A high ranking officer in the Army who did tours in Korea and Vietnam told me that soldiers with post traumatic stress disorder continue to relive the trauma they experienced in combat because they save their uniforms, photos, and other memorabilia from that time. He recommended that they get rid of everything reminiscent of that time in their lives.

These items create an energetic time warp in which the detrimental emotions and memories hover over all of the occupants in the home. It creates a stuck feeling; an inability to get beyond where you have been in your life, emotionally, intellectually, and spiritually. By clearing your space of these objects, you can release the energy that may be holding you back from moving forward, allowing you to create a healthier vibration in your life.

Additionally by reducing clutter, positive energy is better able to move through the space, revitalizing it. A client called me to do a space cleansing in her home. She said the energy felt "stuck." The family was happy, healthy, and successful in general. As I conducted the ritual around the inside perimeter of the house, I had to step over boxes, storage containers, toys, and piles of clothes to complete the cleansing circuit. While the items were organized in containers and in neat piles, the volume of possessions filling the space created the **stuck** feeling the client noticed. Once the cleansing was completed, I asked the client if she and her husband felt tired and had difficulty concentrating when they were home. Her eyes grew large and she exclaimed, "Yes!" I told her it was due to the items blocking the flow of energy through the house. Later, they built an addition that gave them some relief, and also purged quite a few items.

Creating a space through the release of emotions and objects that have outlasted their usefulness allows the entrance of new energy that is timely to your process. If no space is made, no new energy can come in, and the stuck feeling persists. Once again, we manifest externally that which is prominent within us. As you release outdated emotions, assume an attitude of gratitude and forgiveness. Once this occurs, you will be more willing to let go of those objects that symbolize the old and unproductive.

At times, objects may choose to eliminate themselves from your life. Sometimes, when the owner of an object experiences an energetic shift to a higher vibrational pattern, the object that holds the lower vibrations of a negative circumstance or person will break or remove itself in some other way. Objects that carry the low vibrational patterns of negative energy have difficulty withstanding a strong flow of the higher vibrations that come with positive thought and action.

Here is an example of this dynamic. There was a woman involved in an unhealthy relationship. When the ties between her spouse and her were severed, she took with her possessions acquired during that relationship. With each hostile memory from that period she forgave, an item broke "accidentally." The Universe was giving her a signal that she had successfully shed another layer of hindering thoughts and beliefs developed during that time that holds negativity to her.

Other symbols of that relationship were gradually demolished. The building where the wedding took place was leveled. She heard the news on the day she realized that it had been necessary to go through such disruption and emotional upheaval in order to learn the lesson of dealing with obstruction. She felt lighter each time she shed an object from that era. Additionally, she keeps her home clear by regularly purging her possessions. She removes clothing, crockery, decorations, and any item that has gone unused for at least one year, from the space to allow bright new energy to come in.

In extreme circumstances, the Source Energy may block you from owning an object that you have a strong desire to possess. The reason is that there is another object, of which you are most likely unaware, that is more suitable for your purpose.

To illustrate this point, I can share a situation that happened to me with a statue I ordered for my garden. It was of The Huntress, my namesake and goddess of the moon. She had beside her a loyal dog, which for me represented my special being, Mai Tai, whose spirit had passed on. I found her by searching for hours on the Internet, finding a garden store that represented her manufacturer, and special ordered her, along with a pedestal to display her. It seemed the perfect centerpiece for my garden.

The store told me that she would arrive in three months. Three months passed and the day finally came when they called to tell me she had arrived. We scheduled a delivery appointment, and I arranged to be home at that time. The day before she was scheduled for delivery, I received a call from the store telling me that there had been an accident with the statue and that it would be best if I came down to see if I still wanted it.

When my husband and I got there, we saw her standing there with two chunks broken off the drape that was her gown. Her loyal canine companion was missing his hip and leg. As perfect as I felt the statue had been, the Universe had intervened to let me know that its energy was not what was needed in that space. I rejected the statue and did not reorder.

A few months later, I came across the powerful presence of a brand new, four-foot high brass Tibetan Buddha statue. It felt right the moment I saw it. The store even gave a generous discount. Now it sits on a circular slate patio, bringing peace and wisdom to the space in a way the other statue never could.

Natural Materials

Objects made of natural materials such as crystals hold a particularly intense form of energy. The electromagnetic field around crystals can be measured using scientific instruments. The field around a particular stone or crystal can vary depending upon its size, shape, color, and density. Different types of gems and minerals emanate certain properties inherent to that particular stone. Darker stones feel energetically heavier and tend to be used for grounding and protection;

clear or light colored stones have a higher frequency and are generally used for healing and energy amplification.

Clear quartz is a good mineral to use when seeking to amplify a particular vibrational pattern. Take care in the use of this crystal. For example, use clear quartz in your home office to amplify the creative flow for writing and other work. At the same time, it would be foolhardy to bring one into a general office environment where the energy comes from many people and most likely, not the type of energy you would want to amplify. Unless the stone is charged for a particular purpose, it will amplify whatever is around it, whether it is positive or negative, so it is important to be aware of the type of energetic field you are enhancing.

Keep in mind the various properties of the stones you choose to wear and carry. Consider what types of situations and people you may be encountering on a particular day and prepare yourself accordingly, using the stones most likely to have a positive impact on the circumstance. Diamonds are good as overall aura cleaners and can amplify the energy around you similarly to the clear quartz crystals. Onyx absorbs negativity and thereby enhances grounding and protection. Wear onyx when you are interacting with any type of situation or person that tends to be energy draining. It will limit the amount of negative energy that enters your body's energy field.

Clustered crystals create an energy pattern to beam out positive energy, to enhance the energy that is already within the space, or to draw a certain type of energy to you. Rose quartz is used to bring in a calming, loving vibration either into your home or to you personally by wearing or carrying a piece with you.

Stones imbedded into metals such as gold and silver hold their own unique vibrational patterns. Individuals sense these patterns in a variety of ways. Gold vibrates to the sun and gives off a forceful and direct energy, while silver vibrates to the moon, and its influence is more subtle, softer, and magical. Its energy feels lighter and easier to channel. Be aware of how you experience the energetic patterns of silver and gold. These interpretations may vary depending on culture or tradition. Given your own interpretation of their energy patterns, determine when it would be most auspicious to wear it.

As a thorough discussion of this topic is beyond the scope of this book, I recommend Melody's book *Love Is in the Earth* or *The Book of Stones* by Robert Simmons and Naisha Ahsian for a comprehensive list of stones and their metaphysical properties.

Clearing Objects

It is a good idea to clear any item you have decided to bring into your personal space. Even brand new items can hold undesirable energy from all of the adventures it experienced during manufacturing and shipping. Depending on the materials the object is made of, you can choose a variety of ways to clear its energy. With all methods, focus your intent on removing all negativity and clearing the object of any harmful vibrations.

- **Sea Salt** is an excellent general cleanser and can be used on minerals and non-corrosive surfaces. Either mix the sea salt in water and pour it over the object or use it dry and bury or surround the object in sea salt.
- **Full Moon or Sunlight** is a good method for any type of object. Place the object outside under the light of the moon or sun for several hours.
- **White Sage** purifies any object. Put the sage in a metal bowl or seashell and light it. Blow on it gently to put out the flames and allow it to smolder. Wave the object over the burning sage and allow it to be engulfed in cleansing smoke.
- **White light** can be beamed from your hand onto the object. Envision the object immersed in bright white light displacing any unwanted energies. If you have had a Reiki attunement, use the beaming techniques taught to you during your certification. If not, see the section on directing energy (pp. 126 - 135).

Depending on the type of energy emanating from the object, you may want to remove it from your presence altogether. Try to gauge how you feel emotionally and physically when you are around the object to determine if the energy is helpful or harmful, and then act accordingly. If you would like to keep the item, clear its current energy pattern and then charge it to your will.

Charging Objects

Many people carry what they deem as a "good luck" charm; a rabbit is foot, lucky penny, prayer card, or an angel pin. The desire for protection from physical and psychic attack is one reason charms such as these have been persisted for centuries. Luck implies success by chance. The good luck charm enhances the odds for the owner, assisted by the owner's belief in the charm.

When the object is charged for a specific purpose it is deemed a talisman; an object designed specifically for protection is called an amulet, such as a St. Christopher medal, Italian horn, or Christian cross. Storing the talisman or amulet with objects of like energy intensifies the effect. For example, a talisman charged to draw money to the wearer, when stored in a box lined with green fabric and containing coins, aventurine, and other personal symbols of money, wealth, and abundance, will enhance its properties. Grouping items that belonged to a loved one intensifies the vibration felt from them. There are times you may want to amplify this vibration or minimize it. The strategy of grouping items amplifies the energy using objects of a similar energy pattern. In this way, the objects will create an energy transfer one to the other and intensify the vibrational pattern's effect on the space.

Charge jewelry worn for protection to deflect negative thoughts, desires, and actions of others. Jewelry charged to maintain the light around the auric field allows the wearer to avoid feeling depleted during intense interactions. Silver and gold work well to provide protection, especially when imbedded with stones like lapis lazuli. Wearing several pieces at once increases the effects.

Charge any number of items to your special purpose: clothing, jewelry, and miscellaneous objects are all appropriate to use as talismans. To identify an object you wish to charge, begin by sensing the energy of the things you wear and carry. Do you attribute a special protective vibration to any of them? Is there a new object you would like to turn into a protective amulet? Is there an antique of some sort you would like to select for your purpose?

In making your selection, consider the energy it will take to intensify its charge. It will take less energy on your part to charge an object that has been with you the longest or the most consistently; it has been absorbing your vibrational pattern over time. Both new objects and antique (formerly owned by someone other than you) need to be first cleared of the vibrations of all they have come in contact with. The challenge with the old object is in clearing it of any malevolent energy, while maintaining any positive vibrations that are imprinted on it. In the case of the brand new object, it can be easier to charge with a specific purpose or desire, yet it is difficult to determine how much energy the object will need to absorb for it to be effective.

Without formal ritual, the charge of a stone's field can be tuned by the person using it, wearing it, or possessing it. Jewelry made from precious metals can be made powerful by the owner. They are excellent conductors of energy and so are charged with the wearer's dreams and desires. A ring, for example, will absorb the tendencies, characteristics, and emotions of the person who wears it most often. The information is stored within the ring, creating an information layer about the person. People who are sensitive to the energies imprinted on objects are called psychometrists. Some individuals have such strong energy that they imprint the object with a field that feels thicker than normal, allowing the average person to be able to detect a presence.

To charge an object with specific intent, hold it in your most energetically tuned hand, that is, whichever hand projects the strongest energy. Close your eyes and concentrate on the desire you have for the object. For example, if you want to imprint a green candle to have the energies of bringing money to you, hold the candle and picture money falling from the sky and surrounding you, envision providing wonderful service in exchange for the money, and smile as you see your wealth grow in your mind's eye. Ask for the specific amount of money you require. Always ask for your desires to manifest with harm to none. Afterward, light the candle to release the money energy.

Perform the same process with any object. Be clear with your intent and desire as you hold the object. Phrase your intent in present tense, as though it was already true, such as "This object bears the vibration of success, prosperity, and abundance for all of my endeavors, with harm to none." It is best to imprint objects with positive affirmations and always with harm to none. Remember, whatever energy you put out into the Universe comes back to you threefold.

Places and Energy

Houses, buildings, meadows, wooded areas, beaches, and almost any place else you can think of have energies associated with them. They may be vibrations of joy and success or they may hold energy of a sinister nature. The type of energy that resides in an indoor space depends on the people who have been there, the activities that have occurred, and the objects in that space. The building may also be affected by energies left on the land itself from what transpired there prior to the space being built.

Some outdoor areas have an ominous feel to them, especially isolated natural areas. The combination of certain trees, rocks, and water can create energies that raise the spirit or diminish it. There are legends of forests with areas that harm or heal. Each species of tree has distinctive energies associated with it. For example, a grove surrounded by oak trees with the associated energy of strength may feel safe. On the other hand, an area occupied by blackthorn, used by the Celts as a barrier against humans entering a location, may feel menacing. It could also be the case that something took place in a natural area that imprinted it with joy or with suffering.

I have explored woods all over the United States, including the redwood forests of California, the amazing woodlands of Oregon, the magnificent deciduous forests of Pennsylvania, and the tropical growth of Florida and North Carolina. In general, it is an uplifting and energizing experience. The exception was an expanse of forest in a state park in Maryland. I was with my advanced energetics students, and we were looking for a location to hold class. We parked and began walking the trails near a pond. I expected to find an ideal spot that was energetically supportive of our work together. We walked for much longer than anticipated, feeling a sense of unease the entire time. I checked in with them, and they were feeling the same way. The deeper into the woods we walked, the more restless we felt, so decided to turn around and go back towards the parking area. We tried a trail that had been overlooked going into the forest and found a small spot that felt calm. It felt odd to feel so uncomfortable walking in the woods, for that was the first time it had happened to me. In discussing what we felt, there were a few theories that included potential criminal activity of some sort, but no historical information to validate our impressions. We put these thoughts behind us, cleared ourselves and the space of the disquieting energies and set intentions for the work at hand.

Types of Energetic Imprints in Physical Spaces

When you enter a place for the first time, notice how you feel. Energetic imprints left in physical space affect your aura and can have an uplifting or detrimental effect on your energy. Do you feel anxious or agitated? Do you feel calm and serene? Do you feel nothing at all? Now focus your attention on the energy of that space. Try to determine what you are feeling and from where the sensation originates. Respond to the way you are feeling and either remain or depart.

Toxic Places

Places have energetic imprints from those who have been there recently or in the past, depending on the strength of the experiences. Some places evoke a feeling of discomfort—this occurs when there is an imbalance between negative and positive energy. When negative energy is present, it can cause anxiety, fatigue, depression, and anger. Places like prisons and psychiatric hospitals take on malevolent energies due to the residents' psychological and emotional states, the torment they experience, the violence that occurs, and the attitudes of the staff. The vibrations of the activities that take place there occur repeatedly and imprint onto the ether that permeates the environment. Any place that has particular types of activities or inhabitants takes on that specific energetic profile. Places of worship have a distinctive atmosphere, as does a slaughterhouse, a mortuary, a battlefield, or a hospital.

Places like bars, where there is a sense of desperation, depression, and loneliness coupled with the central nervous depressant effects of alcohol, hold within them agitated energy. This type of energy promotes sudden bursts of anger, inappropriate sexual conduct, and behaviors that would most likely not occur outside of this environment. For those who are empathic or energetically sensitive, the energy of loud, crowded places is especially upsetting and disruptive, and it is recommended they avoid these types of environments, lest they become energetically imbalanced as a result.

At the opposite end of the spectrum, a library holds quiet, contemplative energy that is conducive to learning, studying, and the cultivation of wisdom. The books themselves have energies all their own and the patrons revel in the serenity the library bestows.

Avoid visiting places where torture, death, murder, and violence of any kind have taken place. The energies will interact with your personal energies and affect your overall well-being. Those with strong auric fields will experience less of a negative effect than those who are mentally, physically, spiritually, or emotionally weak. Take protective steps to lessen the influence of these energies if you must expose yourself to this type of location (see the section on fortifying and protecting your energetic body pp. 33 - 44).

Dwellings

Energy can imprint onto dwellings. People make dwellings what they are. Consider how a residence takes the energy of those who live there. If the residents feel depressed and hopeless, the building they live in will begin to deteriorate. The surroundings absorb their energy, thereby manifesting the nature of the people who live or work there. Worn and shabby buildings house those who are not living to their potential. The inhabitants have no care for themselves, or for their property. The vegetation surrounding the property begins to consume the house, shrouding it in darkness and perpetuating the low vibrations of the people who live inside. To clarify, this is not a function of lacking money, but rather an outward manifestation of low vibrational level and self-esteem.

Another indicator of the energetic profile of a dwelling is the behavior and condition of the animals that live there. Animals are acutely sensitive to energy and react according to their environments. If the pet is hyper and anxious, there are disruptive energies in the space, most likely emanating from the humans living there. If not from the pet parents, then there could be agitation coming from an imprinted energy from the past, such as the lingering energies of those that lived there before or who have passed away. When the pets are calm and serene, they are reflecting the energy of the home and its occupants.

Some places have no energy at all. I went to visit the newly purchased home of a friend. I brought sage and prayer to bless the home for balance and protection. He gave me a tour. Throughout the home, I noticed a marked lack of energy. It was as if it was a brand new house, yet a family of four had lived there for two years before my friend bought it. When I mentioned what I was picking up, he confirmed that when he first saw the house, the family was still living there. He said that even then, it was sparsely furnished and felt empty. It is unusual to leave no energetic impression whatsoever. I did not perform the cleansing, because there was no energy to modify. This is quite rare and was the only time I encountered such a total absence of energy in a space.

Sometimes the emotional despondence of a dweller brings down the energy of a space. A woman I know was going through a difficult time and was feeling very depressed. She asked me to do a space cleansing to help lift the energy of her home. When I arrived, the apartment had a gray hue to the air, despite the sunlight coming in the window and the colorful wall paint. Even her cats seemed lethargic. After clearing it with sage and prayer, we went out for about an hour. Upon returning, the apartment was brighter and felt lighter than it had before, even though it was dark outside.

In the same way that the woman's depression had turned the energy of her residence gray, you are imprinting on your workplace and personal space every day. Your office/work area and home/bedroom have certain vibrations to them that others can sense. Take stock of what you bring into your space and what you are projecting into it. Keep the vibrational frequency high; sitting in dense energy all day, or even sleeping in it, is like bathing in mud, putting a dull coating onto your auric field.

Ethereal Presence

Residents who have died leave an imprint of their lives on the dwelling. Some have crossed over, yet you can feel their presence, sometimes in the form of emotions, in particular rooms of the house. Traumatic events imprint on the space and sometimes manifest as ghostly activity or a deep heaviness in the environment. Sometimes, the imprint is a sort of memory of the event running as a continuous loop, replaying over and over. People with the gift of energetic sight are able to watch the imprint. These events are truly energetic imprints and are differentiated from other types of apparitions that have their own volition, actively participating in the present despite their disembodied state.

When a person dies and the spirit remains in the home or other space, its presence may lead to certain occurrences. You may sense these lingering energies as a feeling of being watched, a tingle on your skin, a sudden change in temperature, such as cold spots, a density to the air, unexplained noises, or doors opening or closing for no apparent reason. There may also be emotional reactions on the part of the current occupants of the dwellings, such as a feeling of sadness or generalized depression.

An example of this is a case where the living resident of a historic manor home was experiencing footsteps in the middle of the night, pressure on her bed, and extreme, uncharacteristic depression since renovations had started on the home. Making structural changes to a dwelling can trigger the release of dormant energies, taking on the characteristics of a haunting. The contractors were reluctant to work on the project. Her dogs reacted with much agitation. Her discomfort with these disturbances prompted her to call me to perform a space cleansing.

I prepared for the space cleansing by clearing myself of all negativity, grounding, donning black clothing, and wearing a protective amulet. Armed with a sage wand, Holy Water, and prayer, I entered the home and immediately felt the oppressive energy. Throwing holy water at the foyer, I said a prayer, lit the sage wand, and began my trek of the entire inside perimeter of the three-story mansion, including the basement. As I extolled the virtues of The Source, the sage smoke billowed, inserting a higher vibration than the low-level energies of the malefic spirit. The oppressive energy lightened but did not completely dissipate.

The house was so large that it took a couple of hours to get to the third floor. The presence felt most prevalent on this level. Moving through the heavy energy, I completed the blessing of the third floor and began to descend the staircase when a wall of dense energy blocked me mid-step. The sage wand sparked furiously, the embers burning the hand that held it as though the spirit was trying to make me drop the smoking weapon. Sage wands generally do not throw sparks, so this was highly unusual. I held onto the sage wand and pushed through it, using potent prayer, and evoking protective energies. Making my way to the first floor, I was glad to have successfully faced the challenge presented on the third floor staircase.

The client felt lighter, her depression subsided, and the frequency of the occurrences lessened but did not completely end. The renovations were completed. The dogs had a more subdued reaction to the presence. The cleansing took the edge off the presence but did not completely dispel it. We think that the spirit of the original owner of the home created the energy, and he felt that the current owner was changing his abode and invading his territory, so he made it uncomfortable to live there.

Exercise 4-2: Practice Sensing Energy

> Check how you feel in certain places, rooms, or areas. Walk from room to room. Is there a difference in what you feel? Who has been there before you? Are you sensing their energies or the energies of the space alone? What occurred in the past that may have imprinted there?
>
> Now ask someone to walk into your space and share their impressions of the energy there. Is their perception of your energy what you expected? How would you like it to feel? Take steps to shift the energy in your personal and work spaces to make them more attractive to positive and supportive types of energies.

Cleansing a Space

To raise the energy of a place or space, perform a ritual cleansing, followed by an activity that brings joy into the space—a party or celebration—with positive, happy people enjoying themselves. Their pleasure blesses the space with happiness and abundance. The purpose of a house warming party is to bring warmth and joy into the space. It is a way to raise energy in the space with the force of many human spirits. You can do this when moving to a new place, after a renovation, or to bring new energy into your existing space. Knowing the impact the energy of others has in your space, it is wise to consider the nature of the people you choose to invite into your personal environment. Avoid those who are jealous or critical and invite those who bring positive energy into your home or work environment.

Perform a cleansing whenever you feel a location needs it. Symptoms that tell you the space needs clearing include a heavy feeling in the air, unusual or more frequent moodiness of the people living there, a stretch of "bad luck," or any other type of disruption taking place. A spiritual cleansing of a home or sacred space, whether it is done indoors or outdoors, removes negative energy that may cause disruptions or distractions. In essence, you are clearing and blessing the space to make it a much more pleasant place to live, work, or use. There are many ways to perform ritual cleansings. Here are two that I use. Feel free to try these, use another method, or create your own technique. Keep the purpose of calming, balancing, and clearing the space in mind regardless of which option you choose.

Before beginning either of the following methods:

1. Cleanse yourself mentally, emotionally, and physically. For the physical cleansings, take a shower and use a sea salt scrub with peppermint or take a hot bath with sea salts. For the mental and emotional aspect, as you bathe, picture all frustrations, annoyances, and disappointments leaving you and pouring down the drain along with the dirty water. You can also use the "dumping" method described in the clearing and grounding section (pp. 24-28).

2. Put on comfortable, fresh, clean clothes. Light-colored, natural fabrics work well in most cases. When performing the cleansing ritual for highly negative activity, it is best to wear black clothing to protect yourself from whatever is causing the disruption.

3. See yourself surrounded by white light and beam it out as far as you can. This protective shell will serve to allow you to complete the ritual safely.

4. Picture whatever force will be helping you with the cleansing (God, gods, goddesses, watchers, elemental forces, guides, etc.) and ask for assistance.

5. When you arrive at the space you will be cleansing, take a moment to meditate on your purpose for being there. Take several deep breaths and let all tension leave you. Open a window or two to let out any accumulated negative energy.

Fragrance-free Method

For those who are sensitive to smells and fragrances, I recommend the energetic cleansing technique using energy and prayer. Enter the room and position yourself in the doorway, giving you the best vantage point to see the entire room. Envision white light filling every corner of the room while speaking a prayer you choose or write yourself invoking positive intention, abundance, and joy. Make the white light as bright as possible; let it fill the space and your body. You can imagine the white light surrounding you or beam it out from your hands. Feel joy in your heart and, if so called, the energy of Source coming in through the top of your head (crown chakra) and filling you with love and light. Go room to room and repeat this procedure.

Sage Method

This simple smudging method that has worked for me over the years.

Materials

- A bell, gong, drum, or cymbal (optional)
- Holy Water (optional)
- Sage oil mixed with distilled or pure water in an atomizer (used instead of burning materials for those with smoke allergies)
- Sage—sagebrush or white sage, depending on personal preference
- Sweet grass braid to mix with the sage or hang over a doorway to bless those who enter
- Cedar, copal, or sandalwood to mix with the sage
- Any other herbs that you feel would clear and bring positive energy into the space

Blue sage looks like brown twigs bundled together and gives off a sweet fragrance. It symbolizes Grandmother Energy and cleanses negativity. White sage looks like a bundled bunch of grayish dried leaves. It symbolizes protective Grandfather Energy. Both are good to use in the cleansing ritual, depending upon your personal preference. I use a combination of the two, mixed with copal, cedar, and Sweet grass.

Step-By-Step Instructions for Ritual Cleansing

1. Starting at the front door the home or space, sprinkle Holy Water and say, "God's peace be in this home and in all who live here." (Optional, but recommended.)
2. Light the sage and/or combination of ingredients (loose or wand). When you see it glow, blow out the flame. Use a shell or fireproof bowl to burn the sage and/or catch the ashes to avoid burning anything. Substitute sage spray for smudge when necessary.

3. If you would like, ring the bell, chime, or cymbal or beat the drum, to signal the beginning of the ritual. Sometimes I use my drum, which has a deep, resonant sound. The sound is also a form of cleansing; the tone helps clear away unwanted energy, but is not enough in and of itself to completely clear a space.

4. Pick up the sage wand and, beginning at the entrance of the house or other space, move counterclockwise through the space. This direction is called "wittershins" and is the direction used for banishing unwanted energy. [Note: some prefer to move clockwise when performing space cleansing. I move clockwise, especially when using the combination sage wand with Sweet grass. Use whichever direction feels right to you.] Move along the entire inside perimeter of the home, waving the smoldering sage wand up and down or in a circular motion to allow the smoke to permeate the area. Outline windows and doorways, open closets and cabinets, to insure that there is no place for the negative energy to hide. As you wave the wand, say your favorite psalm or prayer throughout the ritual.

5. If the home has more than one floor, follow the wall and proceed to the upper floors and down the stairs into the lower level. Continue to follow the wall until you end at the front door.

6. Pick up the sweet grass braid (if you have not used it in the mixture you burned) and move around the perimeter once again, this time in a clockwise direction. Imagine light reaching to every corner of the space.

7. At the end of this portion of the cleansing, thank whatever Powers helped you to clear the space and declare that this space is now filled with love, light, peace, and happiness.

8. In between cleansings, keep the area clear by burning cedar, copal, or sandalwood incense and by being thankful for the many wonderful things in your life.

Designing a Space with Energy

A fun way to use your energetic awareness is to create unique designs in a space using the energy flow both indoors and out. In the same way you sense energy from people and places, apply it to the area you wish to create or modify. The study of Feng Shui is useful to acquaint yourself with the concept of promoting auspicious energy flow to the space and ways to overcome energetic obstacles. As with all forms of energetic philosophy, it has many variations of the rules depending on the perspective and tradition of the practitioner or author. Use the Feng Shui methods you feel best align with your beliefs and couple that with your own intuitive sense of the energy in a space regarding what needs to be changed to promote maximum flow.

Start by identifying a space such as the living room. Stand in the doorway facing into the room. Scan it using all of your senses, including what you feel energetically. Try to sense how the energy is moving in the space. Now move into the room and walk a path that feels natural. How do guests move through the space when they visit? Does it feel like a natural path or does it feel blocked or forced? Consider how furniture and accessories allow the flow of energy or block it. For example, a sofa positioned across a doorway blocks the energy from coming into the room. Turn the sofa so that it no longer cuts across the doorway and feel the difference in the energy coming to the space. Clutter severely diminishes the energy moving through the space, so remove excess objects and purge regularly.

Outdoors, look into the designated space and notice the naturally created energy patterns. Start by scanning the environment for patches where bare earth peeks through the vegetation; this could outline a natural walking path or sitting area. The shape of a hill may suggest where to place steps. Feel the plants around you to mark where the energy feels strongest. If the plants or trees are doing well in the existing location, allow them to remain in the space. Once the hardscape area is established, then determine plant placement. Close your eyes and envision the garden the way you want it to appear when it is completed. Test the energy mentally to see if it feels right to you.

Curved shapes promote meandering energy rather than forceful energy that flows too harshly down straight lines. Do not base your plantings solely on ruler measurements; accommodate any variation that you feel in the ground as you go to plant. Try to sense if the plant will thrive in that spot or if it would be better to dig a hole a couple inches in a different direction. Existing vegetation will give you a sense of where new plantings will thrive.

Be gentle with the area so as not to upset its natural balance. Try to enhance it rather than change it. Too much disruption in the surrounding area may change the vibration of the outdoor space. If you start with a spot that feels harmonious, that is, in harmony within itself, then try to minimize the devastation of the area as you go to plant.

When I designed my garden, it was a blank slate of grass surrounded by mature sycamore and maple trees. There was a natural swale that channeled water from my neighbors' homes, through my yard, and into the creek. Rather than disrupt the natural flow of the water, I enhanced it by placing large white stones into it to minimize erosion. The flagstone paths were designed to flow into each other, and the plantings were done at the end to beautify the experience of walking on the pathways. The Buddha I mentioned earlier sits in a flagstone circle and is backed by clumping bamboo. The colors I chose were purple, white, and pink and selected plants that would thrive in my zone, as well as bring the desired energy into the space. Roses, peony, vinca, yarrow, and May night salvia have grown healthy and co-existed harmoniously over the years. Additional tree plantings of Japanese maple and Kousa dogwood have also succeeded by having their locations chosen energetically. The overall result is a peaceful space that is harmonious and energizing.

When planning your garden, feel the energy flow of the ground, as well as the flow that you would like to create. Come up with a plan that weds the two in a harmonious way. Feel the energy that moves within the space you are planning. A pendulum comes in handy when determining the direction of energy in a space. Hold the pendulum over the area and see how it swings. Does it flow from east to west or north to south? When you gaze across the yard, where does your eye move? Is there a particularly lovely spot that you want to preserve as it is? What can you do to enhance that spot?

Once you have a basic sense of energy flow indoors or out, you will be able to place furniture, design a garden, raise the energy, or modify a space simply guided by your intuition. You will see what is needed for balance and harmony at an energetic level. Top it off by doing a space cleansing and/or beaming white light into the space.

Chapter 5 – Magickally Create Your Reality: The Power of Perspective Change

You are a magickal being, able to transform your reality at will. Reality is what you perceive it to be. Everything you encounter and *observe is subjected to your own perspective and filtered through your* experience, thereby creating a personal version of what it means. I call this *Phenomenological Truth*, and it is experienced by each individual on the planet.

How we experience reality and ultimately what we consider as our truth is subjective. While certain human experiences are universal, such as emotions—joy, grief, depression, anxiety—and physical responses—pain, pleasure, hunger—the individual perspective drives when these emotions manifest; many times what is considered physically pleasurable to one person may not be to another. Pain thresholds vary. Each of us reacts to life differently; what stresses one person is stimulating to another.

We also create our reality by the way we look at the world. When we choose to experience life as a great adventure, it is one; when we choose to look at everything as a problem, then life is hard. To change our reality, our truth, and our range of experience, we simply need to change our perspective. Each person comes into the world with their own unique gift and purpose and then is subjected to a variety of experiences and encounters, which ultimately shape and direct the person's actions, thoughts, and understanding. This is what makes the Phenomenological Truth the most compelling.

What we focus on becomes our truth. If one person chooses to focus on all the struggles of the world, then their truth is that the world is a dangerous and difficult place. If another person chooses to see that personal and societal struggles are a mechanism by which to learn and move past difficulties, then their truth is a world filled with opportunities to improve.

Psychology, philosophy, scientific, and metaphysical schools of thought support this perspective. Truth shifts and changes depending on who is experiencing the situation. Look at research on any topic. You can pick a subject and find a study that says it is true, one that says it is false, and one that says no definite conclusion can be drawn. The design of the research study is a function of the researcher's perspective on finding the truth about a particular subject. The tools and mechanisms used to uncover the truth about the subject may influence the outcome of the study. How we choose to measure the phenomenon limits our ability to find the truth. In physics, we know that the potential of a particle is unlimited until it is observed, and then it is fixed in its observed state.

The number of variables considered, the perspective of the person analyzing the available data, and the depth of relevant knowledge the person has all modify the truth derived from that experience. At any point, we have no idea what piece may be missing from the equation; therefore, it is difficult to be confident that our conclusions are accurate for all people. What is important here is that it is accurate for ourselves and how our conclusions affect the way we choose to move through life.

Transforming Your Reality

Irrational thoughts and beliefs need to be identified and challenged in order to grow and change. Anxiety comes from harboring perceptions that produce a negative view of the Self and the environment. It is at this time that people utilize their ego-defense mechanisms to provide relief from anxiety. A common defense is denial, which allows the person to repress painful circumstances, uncomfortable thoughts, or their role in making life what it is. They then replace it with a story they create that feels acceptable to them. Defenses serve to deny and distort reality, at times promoting the individual's avoidance of what they need to face up to. It is important to note that ego-defenses do not help resolve the core of the conflict, which is to know oneself and to find a sense of purpose and meaning. Once that is found, anxiety is alleviated.

Your reality can be transformed by gaining a new perspective on a past experience. Changing perspectives allows the freedom to relearn behaviors that were a direct result of the false perspective. The true lessons become attainable and can be used to gain understanding of the self. Once the lesson is learned, it is then time to move on to the next phase.

As we go through various stages in our lifetime, each is important because we must build on what was previously learned. This viewpoint does much to destroy guilt and judgment about oneself and to encourage objective consideration of what transpired. It is important that the experience is remembered accurately, in the feelings and thoughts that revolved around the perceptions of the experience. To understand that patterns of behavior learned early in life are being repeated in the present is to understand that the original lesson has not yet been learned.

Once the true meaning of the experience is realized, there is no longer a need to control the anxiety that is produced by distorted lessons. By understanding each experience and its place in your development, you will become more accepting of all experiences, both positive and negative. It is never too late to understand the teachings of previously unlearned lessons and how you can use them to your benefit.

One thing I do know is true: What my world looks like is completely up to me. I choose to see a beautiful world, filled with opportunity, where anything is possible. It is never too late to change our perspective. We are always at the beginning. We are all a work in progress...

Exercise 5-1: Explore Your World View

Take out your journal and ask yourself the following questions:
- What does your world look like?
- Do you believe that people are inherently good or generally malign?
- Do you expect and prepare for the worst or do you trust that everything will work out for the best? Maybe some of both? What does it depend on?
- What does your ideal world look like?
- How big is the gap between what it looks like today and what you want it to be?

Change Your Perspective & Shift the Energy

Our perspective is the result of everything we have concluded based on what we have experienced. It is our interpretation of ourselves and our circumstances and the associated meanings we apply to them. Perception and memory carry with them the energy associated with that memory. The energy of the associated memory is just as powerful as the actual experience. This is the basis of disorders such as post traumatic stress disorder (PTSD), which carries with it a sense of reliving the trauma over and over again, including all of the sensations, emotions, and imagery that occurred under the original circumstances.

You record events into memory from childhood onward. What is most profound about these recordings is the way you felt during the experience and what that emotion is paired with in the memory. A memory of your father may be paired with joy, love, fear, or resentment. The memory of a school experience may elicit excitement, regret, or embarrassment. These recordings stay with you and continue to influence your reactions to the world, especially when circumstances seem similar to the original event. Depending on your viewpoint, that being in the extreme as positive or negative, you cultivate the density of energetic frequency that coincides with that emotion and corresponding perspective. While most perspectives tend to take the form of a dichotomy, it is valuable to consider neutral perspectives, as in accepting something as "just is" rather than judging it to be "good or bad."

The interpretation you apply to any experience affects beliefs and behaviors. If as a child you see one or both of your parents failing in their efforts, the assumption may be that life is hard and that there is no use in trying; or it can have the effect of striving harder to overcome obstacles and not allow challenges to get in the way of achieving goals. You may have observed your parents or those around you doing everything for others, but never taking care of their own needs. As a result, you may conclude that life is only about giving and never asking for or getting what you need, thereby living in a state of dissatisfaction. Or you may respond by feeling obligated to do things for others, even when you do not want to. Your observations are recorded into memory and associated with a particular emotion, which translates into the vibrational frequency that creates the sense of heaviness or lightness of being.

Exercise 5-2: Childhood Memories

Play some of your memory recordings from childhood. You probably still remember the primary messages from your parents—"Look both ways before you cross the street" or "Do not be childish...grow up!"

What is the number one parental message you remember?

Why is this particularly significant?

Which events stand out in your mind and what are the associated emotions?

Think of the way you felt when you heard the parental message from childhood. How does this affect the way you view the world and yourself today?

Your behavior, choices, and point of view are largely determined by the way you perceive and understand events. Events do not cause behavior, but your perception of those events does. How you feel, think about, and react to current circumstances creates energy around you and the situation you are dealing with. At the same time, energetic residue from past interactions and situations can remain with you, often requiring you to shift your perspective in order to move past it and rid yourself of the stuck energy it creates that is likely to hold you back.

Much of perspective change has to do with your thoughts. Controlling your thoughts is an act of will, to both stop the flow of negative thoughts and to adjust them when they arise. Your will helps in the process of creating new habits of thinking. The key is being aware of the thoughts as they occur and limiting the amount of time you allow them to remain. Reducing the time spent on negative thoughts lessens their energetic hold, thereby taking away their power. By shifting your perspective, the vibrational level of the thought changes.

Raise your personal vibration by replacing negative thoughts about yourself and others with a true statement that increases confidence. For example: "I cannot do anything right"—this may be how it feels, but is likely not accurate (Wing Vibrational Scale Level 5) versus "That mistake allowed me to learn something new"—this is true and provides uplifting energy (Wing Vibrational Scale Level 7). Can you feel the difference? The substituted thought reflects an altered perspective that raised the vibration by two levels.

Be more specific rather than using global statements. Again, using the example of "I cannot do anything right," ask yourself if that is really true, or is it more accurate to say "I'm not very good at this particular thing, but I can do many other things well." Challenge negative thoughts and beliefs with more positive thoughts—using the opposite of the negative or develop an entirely new view on the situation—in order to shift up.

Exercise 5-3: Shifting Perspective

> Grab a frequent negative thought. Now look at it differently. Create a new statement that is true and of a higher vibrational level. Modify global perspective words such as "everything," "always," and "never" and substitute words such as "sometimes." Make your new statement as specific to the situation as possible. Say each statement aloud, both the negative and the new, and see how different they feel from each other. Which one feels better? Rate them on the Wing Vibrational Scale. Were you able to shift the vibrational level higher?

Your perspective also determines the *label* you give to others and vice versa, the label you give something or someone affects the way you perceive it. If you look at someone and think to yourself that that person is a good-for-nothing who cares about no one but himself, then you are likely to treat him with frustration and annoyance. If you look at the same person and think of him as someone who never had the benefit of learning effective communication skills and is quite possibly struggling with low self-esteem, then you are likely to treat him with patience, compassion, and understanding. At the same time, the way other people may be labeling you affects their view of who you are and ultimately treat you accordingly.

Exercise 5-4: Explore Labeling

What labels have you attached lately?

How did they affect your behavior toward the person or situation?

When was the last time you were aware of someone labeling you inaccurately?

How did it change their perception of you?

What could be done to modify that perception?

The will can be used to modify your perspective by using it to evaluate your current beliefs and level of thinking and feeling and then applying it to change specific aspects of these. Seeking to change your perspective can threaten your entire self-perception, and may inhibit the desire or will to make the necessary modification. Anxiety can result when you realize that what is happening cannot be interpreted using your current level of understanding. Guilt surfaces when you do not live up to your self-perception and who you believe yourself to be. The energies of anxiety, guilt, and vulnerability are lower level frequencies and are best kept to a minimum.

To adjust these energies, there must be a willingness to evaluate how you look at the world, as well as to test the validity of the perceptions of others. Once you determine what is actually taking place, you can discard invalid perceptions of self and others. Seeing yourself in a variety of ways rather than from only one perspective allows you to enter into an energetic flow with the ability to shift your point of view, thoughts, and behaviors as needed. Finally, have a desire to continue to stay open to new information that allows you to expand on your sense of self and your role in the world.

Gratitude is one of the best perspective changers. When something unwanted occurs, instead of reacting with guilt and creating drama, challenge the fear, doubt, and worry that drags you down energetically and be thankful for the opportunity to learn something from the situation. It raises both your energy level and vibrational frequency. When your energy goes up, you feel motivated, and can make a plan to overcome issues and obstacles.

You can create a shift through releasing of the old, clearing a space, modifying a belief, learning something new, making a decision, perceiving something differently than you did before, taking control of a situation, or ending or beginning something.

Exercise 5-5: Shifting Energy Within Yourself

> Take stock of your thoughts, beliefs, will, choices/ decisions. Are they aligned with what you envision for yourself? Do they support how you want to move forward or what you want to feel? You can listen to many opinions, read many books, but it comes down to what makes sense for you as an individual. Only you can make choices that are best for you. Your will controls your thoughts, experiences, and actions.

Embrace the Darkness Within

While the light helps us see more clearly, the darkness can help us see more deeply. The dark night of the soul occurs when we cannot feel a connection to Spirit, when we lose our way, or when we find that we have been on the wrong path. In the darkest moments, we can find enlightenment and illumination. The most profound energetic and perspective shifts occur as a result of despair. It helps you to find your center. To descend into this realm affords the opportunity to make shifts not possible when using the light alone. Light burns away certain energies needed to dive into the deep waters as opposed to simply soaring into the sky. Consider the dark energies of suffering, despair, anger, and frustration. Within these dark energies awaits powerful knowledge of the self. These conditions provide the impetus for personal development and self-improvement. They motivate one to take action that overcomes these conditions. The darkness in this case serves as a catalyst for growth. The darkness helps us to reject what is not appropriate to our well-being and serves to show us where we need development. Be aware of how you use the dark forces and know that you will come out the other side stronger and with heightened clarity and resolve.

The dark side of humanity need not be evil; it is a source of power just as love is. The dark force energies allow us to defend, to avoid negativity, to prevent injustice, and to remove energies that do not serve us on our path. Love can create brightness and the dark forces can create personal power that when embraced, acknowledged, and honed, can show us the way to stand up for what we believe and to come more fully into ourselves.

The shadow side of the self must be recognized and mastered so that we cultivate balanced energies within ourselves. When love is deep and someone attacks a loved one, the dark force surfaces to come to our love's defense. Without the dark force, there is no defense, there is no surge of power, and there is no motivation to fight against harm and win. Love's energies have a protective component that can only be released using dark force energy.

Seek to understand both sides. There is no Yin without Yang, no feminine without masculine, no light without the dark. There is a time for expansive joy (Jupiter) and a time for restriction and focus to serious purpose (Saturn). Learn the energies that exist and understand your connection to each. For we all have all energies within us, it is simply a matter of degree. This is not a departure from Source, for Source is comprised of both light and dark. There is no separation, only shades of gray.

Find your center. Sometimes it is in the brightest light and sometimes its place is in the deepest darkness of the soul. To descend into this realm affords the opportunity to make shifts not possible when using the light alone. Light burns away certain energies needed to dive into the deep waters as opposed to simply soaring into the sky.

The universe displays a black matrix with spots of light. Even love has its dark side, such as jealousy or hatred, while darkness has its light by way of defending and protecting. Everything is a blend. Nothing is pure. We are a mixture of all energies. This gives us depth and the ability to create in a multitude of ways. We must know our boundaries as we seek to expand our greatest gifts.

Consider the dark energies of suffering, anger, and frustration. Within these dark energies awaits powerful knowledge of the self. These conditions provide the impetus for personal development and self-improvement. They motivate one to action that overcomes these conditions. The darkness in this case serves as a catalyst for growth and change.

The way you handle a challenge can create a shift. It strengthens your resolve. Surges of power come during times of challenge. Rather than letting external circumstances dictate the ability to cope, conjure your resolve and bolster your strength from the inside. Exude your power and wear it on the outside, projecting it for all to feel.

Exercise 5-6: Practice Raising Your Vibration Level

When you experience a dense energy, such as doubt, fear, or worry, check in with yourself and ask what is motivating you to feel that way. What thoughts or beliefs are generating that frequency? Challenge the thought that is prompting the lower vibration and seek to replace it with a new perspective that will raise your vibrational level. Use your will to sustain this new perspective and maintain the higher energetic vibration.

The darkness is only detrimental when you choose to stay within it and not strive for the glimmer of light that waits on the other side. Do not grieve for what is gone, do not focus on limitation, and do not dwell in resistance to change. Rather, reinvent, reestablish, overcome, and open to new possibilities. Flow with change and release the blocks that prevent you from moving forward.

Define what love means to you. For some it means possessiveness, control, vulnerability, and loss—all stemming from the vibration of fear. Fear that creates these behaviors in the name of love includes fear of change, fear of the unknown, fear of the future, fear of loss, fear of abandonment, fear of death, fear of failure, fear of losing control, and fear of pain. The darkness that blocks the light of love serves to hinder, repel, and destroy. For those who define love as unconditional acceptance and caring, there is a marked absence of fear and an abundance of self-respect, self-love, and trust. Included in this energy is the ability to remove energies that are not for the highest good. Even in love, it is unhealthy to open yourself and repeatedly accept detrimental energies from another with no hope of improvement.

Now define darkness. It has a heavier energy to keep us still and force us to accept responsibility for our actions. By accepting the darkness, we do not expect others to tolerate every decision or behavior we have that may harm them or hold them back. The darkness helps us to reject what is inappropriate to our well-being and serves to show us where we need development. Be aware of how you use the dark forces and understand that whether the energy derives from love or darkness, both have the power to harm and both have the power to heal.

Exercise 5-7: Journaling about Personal Darkness

Think back to a time when you sunk to the darkest depth of yourself. You were in the darkness of depression, grief, or self-doubt.

What did you discover about yourself?

How did you rise above it and resume your life?

Did your life change as a result of the experience? In what ways?

Draw on the power of this experience and use it to understand yourself and to succeed in the face of future challenges.

Create Your Vision

Anyone who is adept at what they do in any capacity starts with a vision. This vision stems from the individual's unique perspective, shaped by their experiences and level of understanding. What one creates and ultimately manifests is a direct reflection of the way one envisions the project, task, or ultimately one's life.

Self-knowledge is critical in this regard, for without it, there is no solid foundational viewpoint from which to create. Your special gifts seek expression. The primary task is to discover what your gifts are. Many think that they possess nothing special within them that anyone would respond to or care about. This simply is not true. So where do you start to discover your vision?

It is a matter of determining your point of view. Consider the program "Project Runway" (2004 –). As you may know, this reality show is a contest among fashion designers to win the chance to start their own clothing line. Each week they get a challenge that frames the fashion design they are to create. No matter what the challenge—to create their own fabrics, to dress a famous person to attend an award ceremony, or to design for children—the judges expect the designers to approach it from their own point of view within the framework of the challenge. This includes how each designer interprets the challenge, uses their sensibilities to choose fabrics, draw their designs, and conceptualize the person for whom they are designing. All of this requires them to draw from their experience, how they view the world, and their skill set. Sometimes, their vision exceeds their abilities and they have difficulty creating what they have in mind. Other times, their own self-doubt inhibits their design and blocks their ability to bring it into reality. The winners generally trust themselves, have a strong vision of the end result, and understand the nature of the challenge.

It is the same with any task: your skills must be in place in order to create what you conceptualize. Your conceptualization is a reflection of your personal viewpoint and understanding of your experience. Any time you approach a problem, perform your daily routine, or determine the best way to complete a task, you are demonstrating your personal perspective. Much of it occurs automatically. Now it is time to pay more attention to what you feel is important and how you choose to deal with it.

Exercise 5-8: Discover Your Point of View

First, ask yourself the following questions:
1. What do I gravitate toward most often?
2. What are my favorite subjects, hobbies, TV shows?
3. What is a common theme that is evident from the first two questions? (For example, you may like shows that are transformational as with home decorating programs that show before and after or makeover shows that transform an individual from frumpy to fabulous. Along these same lines, your hobby may be to refinish furniture, etc.)
4. What do people seek out from me? A skill, advice about something, a supportive shoulder to cry on?
5. What is my passion? What do I enjoy more than anything?
6. What did I like to do as a child?
7. What is my life philosophy?

Now, think about creating something, anything. It could be a building you design or a process to increase efficiency. It can be tangible or intangible.
1. What would it look like?
2. How would you begin?
3. What motivates you to create this?
4. Who would benefit from it?
5. What are you feeling as you think about creating it?

This is the beginning of discovering your point of view; your unique perspective manifesting through the expression of your vision. Once created you can show it to the world, show those close to you, or just demonstrate it to yourself.

Whatever you attempt, whether it is in performing your daily responsibilities, your work, or your personal creative endeavors, put your unique stamp on it, make it your own, and create your vision.

Chapter 6 – Opening To, Drawing, and Directing Energy

We talked about the energy that is within you and how the energy around you impacts your thoughts, feelings, and wellbeing. Now we are going to take control and learn to open to, draw on, and direct energy for your own purposes. Remember that these techniques must always be used ethically and for your highest good and the highest good of all concerned.

Influencing Factors: Diminishing or Increasing Energy

To allow the maximum flow of energy through you, the conduit must be clear. There are several conditions that serve to diminish the amount of energy you are able to move through yourself. These include:

Drugs and alcohol: Central nervous system depressants such as alcohol, marijuana, and painkillers impede the flow of energy through the body. There is a sense of a thickness in the energy field when drugs or alcohol are ingested.

Your diet and overall physical condition impacts how much energy you are able to channel. A diet low in fat, high in fiber, with little to no animal protein, affords ultimate energy flow through the body. Consult your physician before making any changes to your diet.

Fear of letting go or fear of loss prevents you from eliminating the energies created by people and situations that are hindering our progress. This includes those still living and those who have passed on. Some friendships have a purpose in your life for a time, and then both you and the other person need to move on. Generally, the person or situation that moves on is a hindrance to growth and development, so allow its extrication; do not seek to keep it in place. It is not good or bad, it just is. When a particular energy moves out of your life, whether it is a person or circumstance, it is appropriate and timely to your development. There is no need to feel remorse for that which is released for the highest good. It makes room for new energy to come in. Do not be afraid of making room for a positive vibration to enter your life.

Scattered energies: The most powerful interactions are possible when limiting the number of energy sources impacting the situation. If there are many people or conditions involved, the energy expended must be divided between those sources, and then those sources are also divided. It becomes a thread rather than a large pipe. In the work environment, too many variables and conditions affect the efforts of various initiatives, making them less likely to succeed than if the interactions were limited. Scattered energies diminish effectiveness; focused energy creates powerful results.

A sedentary lifestyle is diminishing, because it creates stuck energy that causes physical issues, fatigue, and an inability to attract and channel energy.

To enhance the flow of energy moving through you, the following techniques exponentially increase your energy flow.

Exercise is beneficial in many ways, especially when it serves to move your energy. It can be any activity that allows the body to move for a period of time and release the stuck energy that accumulates from working at your computer or sitting on the couch watching television. Techniques that promote slow, controlled movements like Tai Chi or Yoga increase awareness of where the energy is located and where it goes within the body. Dancing is a wonderful way to move more vigorously and find your natural rhythm. It incorporates the entire body and is an enjoyable way to move energy, build muscle, and shed pounds.

Inner Peace/Mental Calm—The calmer you feel, the more space there is for high frequency energy to move through you. When your mind is filled with constant thoughts and worries, it blocks the flow of energy and wastes the energy you do have on the worry itself. Regularly doing the dumping, grounding, meditation, and protection exercises we discussed earlier will help you achieve and maintain inner calm and peace. This will translate into your external world, as well.

Minimize distractions: Create a space and a mindset where distractions are not allowed. That includes turning off your cell phone and not answering your landline. Stop multitasking and trying to do everything for everyone. Shut down your computer and go someplace where there are minimal people, noise, and movement. Allow yourself to just *be*. It may feel odd at first, you may feel lazy or unproductive, but this is absolutely necessary to get in touch with the energies you are trying to channel and direct.

Elemental Influences on Energy

Natural environments, like the woods or the ocean, recharge your batteries, clear stuck and negative energies, and allow you to connect with the elemental energies of the environment. Once aware of the nature of elemental energies, you see them all around you. Connecting with them gives you a way to strengthen their vibrations.

The element of **Earth** is grounding and is associated with the physical and material aspects of the world. Earth carries with it a sense of dependability and stability. It is connected with all things practical and wise. Caves, canyons, forests, and groves encompass Earth energy. Earth's vibrations also extend into the home, providing comfort and nourishment.

The element of **Air** is the realm of thought and allows movement and change. Air has projective energy that inspires us to move beyond our current state of being. It is a place of new beginnings. Mountaintops, cloudy skies, and windy beaches are places where the vibration of Air lives.

Feel the flame inside of you with the element of **Fire** by gaining understanding of the masculine principle and the energy of the will. Fire is an ancient form of divinity and a symbol of Spirit. Fire purifies and transforms; it creates and destroys. Fire enlightens and is symbolic of the divine light within us. Places associated with Fire are deserts and volcanoes.

When you submerge yourself in the element of **Water**, you dive into the world of the feminine principle, emotions, psychic ability, dreams, and intuition. Water is a passive element with magnetic qualities, able to receive and hold energetic vibrations. Water cleanses and flows, gives life, and is capable of destruction. It is an inspirational force that causes us to reflect, ponder, and create. The fluid nature of Water encourages us to accept diversity and to open to new experiences. It can be tranquil or rough and so represents emotions and moods. Places to experience this element include wells, lakes, ponds, waterfalls, rivers, beaches, and the ocean.

Exercise 6-1: Elemental Personality Quiz

Which elemental energies do you resonate most with? Put a check mark in the "agree" or "disagree" box next to each statement. Which element has the most checkmarks? Do you primarily feel closest to one element or another? Are you a combination of several elements? All four elements are represented within your personality. This quiz will reveal to what degree each are represented.

Question	Element	Agree	Dis-agree
I think a while before taking action	Air		
I like looking up into the clouds	Air		
I like feeling a breeze on my face	Air		
I love to learn	Air		
I love to analyze a situation	Air		
I enjoy solving problems	Air		
I handle change well	Air		
Original thinking appeals to me	Air		
I tend to be versatile	Air		
People say I have a lot of good ideas	Air		
I enjoy the comforts of home	Earth		
I prefer a wooded environment	Earth		
People describe me as a grounded person	Earth		
I tend to be a practical person	Earth		
I am a dependable person	Earth		
People consider me to be wise	Earth		
I take care of my body	Earth		
I tend to be patient	Earth		
I tend to be stubborn	Earth		
My material possessions are important to me	Earth		

Question	Element	Agree	Dis-agree
I take action without giving it too much thought	Fire		
I enjoy the desert	Fire		
I like feeling the sun on my skin	Fire		
I feel inspired a good deal of the time	Fire		
I enjoy growing my skills and abilities	Fire		
I am self-motivated	Fire		
I set goals and work to achieve them	Fire		
I tend to be assertive	Fire		
I am an enthusiastic person	Fire		
I generally have willpower	Fire		
I make decisions intuitively	Water		
I prefer to be around lakes or the ocean	Water		
I regularly get intuitive messages	Water		
I tend to be an emotional person	Water		
I consider myself to be creative	Water		
My feelings are easily hurt	Water		
I enjoy nurturing others	Water		
People tell me I am compassionate	Water		
I can feel the emotional pain of others	Water		
My moods go in cycles	Water		
Totals	Air		
	Earth		
	Fire		
	Water		

Overcoming Stuck Energy and Opening to Fresh Energy

Everyone has stuck energy within them now and then. Some people have energies that are imbedded due to repeated negative patterns that cause the energy to stagnate. These energies need to be lifted or released. Let us take a look at how this energy can get stuck and ways to move it.

The Role of Thoughts

The energy that flows around you must be harnessed and dealt with, while the internal energy must be bolstered and transformed. The key to adjusting the energies within you is controlling your thoughts. Thoughts generate emotions and behaviors. Thoughts also create different energy patterns that either increase or decrease your capacity to deal with people, events, and life in general. Hard to change patterns of behavior are the result of an inability to change the flow of energy in yourself. This energy is stuck, unable to change or expand from its current form. An increased awareness of your energy flow can help you learn when energy is stuck and what is keeping it that way.

One of the most frequent causes of stuck energy is complaining. Even those who claim they have let go of a situation keep energy moving in the same pattern if they bring it up time and time again and complain about it, all the while feeling the same level of aggravation they felt the first time. If instead, the belief or thought is shifted to a fresh perspective on the topic, the pattern is able to be interrupted, and a new thought/energy pattern can be created. I have witnessed what I call the Endless Loop Complex when people repeatedly complain about a particular relationship with their significant other, family member, or job. It always consists of the same components—how the situation hurts them, how it is unfair, how frustrated they are—but never during an Endless Loop discussion does it include how to move past it, how they can change the way they think about it, or how they can look for a new situation that is more appealing.

The same thoughts create the same energies moving in the same directions. The hamster-wheel effect transpires when the thoughts go round and round. The low vibrational level it brings is maintained, the complainer is exhausted, and so are the people around him/her. There are three simple steps to breaking free of this pattern and opening to fresh new energies. First, stop complaining. Each time you catch your-self saying the same thing, use the rubber band technique and stop the flow of negativity. Then take a hard look at what you are really complaining about. You become what you focus on, so make sure the energy you put into your thoughts is aligned with what you want to be and what you actually want in your life.

If you have a difficult relationship with your significant other, is it really about your self-worth? If you are at odds with your boss, is the underlying issue that you really dream of having your own business and a regular job seems to be holding you back? If you argue with your parents, are you being given the opportunity to see them as regular people with their own issues or are they bringing your self-doubt to the forefront? Finally, make a change to shift out of the same thought patterns that create the same behaviors and energies that ultimately keep you stuck. Even one small change can break the pattern. This can result in a significant shift sufficient to keep the flow going in the direction in which you really want to head. Take action to resolve, modify, or eliminate the source of the complaint.

Thoughts are also the source of the three deadly enemies—fear, doubt, and worry. It is so easy to get caught up in the *what ifs, shoulds, and cannots;* the cornerstones that hold you back. As we learned, your perspective creates your reality, and if your perspective is that moving forward is scarier than staying miserable, then nothing will change and no opening will occur. If you doubt your ability to make a change and worry what others will think if you make an attempt to achieve your goals, then odds are you will continue the Endless Loop Complex of thoughts that keep you full of anxiety. When these bubble up, ask yourself what you are truly afraid of, doubting, or worried about. Get to the core of the issue.

Exercise 6-2: Opening the Flow of Energy

Identify your number one complaint. What do you complain about most often or bothers you about your life, your relationships, or your job? Write it down. Think about the issues surrounding the complaint in detail. Write it all down. Now take just one point to start, the one that you feel you can have the most impact on, and practice looking at it differently. Write down several different perspectives, whether you initially believe them or not. The key is to change the way you are considering your options and ultimately generate alternatives to the present state of affairs.

For example, your complaint might be "I hate my job." The issues could be that you do not like getting up early in the morning, you do not like the people you work with, and that the work itself holds no interest for you. Alternate perspectives could be that you are grateful for the paycheck you receive so that you can pay your bills while planning a different work option; the people you work with give you the opportunity to experience different types of people, so you are better prepared to deal with them in other situations; and being able to do a mundane job allows you the cognitive bandwidth to use your creative imagination and put your energy toward taking a class or working on a project that interests you outside of work.

If this is not the circumstance you want, what is it that you do want? Write down a positive statement of the way you want things to be in your life and it will open the flow of energy so that your thoughts, behaviors, actions, and energies will align with that desire.

Recognize that you are in control of your life and what is in it. Step out of the victim role and into the driver's seat. Take responsibility for yourself and what you want in your life. You must change the way you are approaching the circumstances that keep you stuck. No one is doing it to you. You are making choices, consciously or unconsciously, and uncovering the motivations behind the choices is necessary to break the pattern. Determine your direction and purpose. This puts everything in context and allows you make choices based on whether or not it takes you closer to your overall goal. Then take action. Do not just dream about what you want; engage in actions that support your desires.

Physical Sensations of Opening

One way to increase awareness and energy flow is to listen to the physical manifestations of this stuck energy, whether it is in the form of intense heartburn (indicating stuck energy in the solar plexus), or headache (stuck in the third eye in the center of the forehead or in the crown chakra at the top center of the head), a heavy sensation in a certain area, etc. Some energetic clogs occur right at the chakra site, while others happen in various parts of the body.

Intense headaches can be caused by stuck energy. (Please note that certain types of headaches require medical attention and should be treated with conventional methods.) A gentleman I worked with complained of a terrible headache that he just could not get rid of with over-the-counter medications. I asked his permission to use Reiki to give him some relief, and he agreed. I felt the energy in his forehead. It was hot and thick, spread across the entire front of his head. I applied energy to the area, and asked him to imagine the pain going into my hand. Without hesitation it leapt from his head and into my hand, where I could dispose of it. He looked at me, shocked, his eyes wide. I asked him how his head felt, and he said that the headache was completely gone. While he had been skeptical of the solution to his pain, he was willing to try it and to let it go.

The energy may be stuck in one of the outer energy bodies rather than in the physical, such as in the emotional or mental layers of your personal energy field. For example, a woman I was working with during a Reiki session requested that I help her release the stuck energy of a failed romantic relationship. I located it just above the left breast. It felt like a sphere of solid, heavy energy. I applied energy to it in an attempt to lift it from her and instead of coming out, it quickly moved to the other side of her chest. I found it once again and applied energy to it, and it went back to the left. That is when I stopped and asked how long it had been since the breakup. She said, "Nine years." She had been holding this pain for nine years and was still not ready to release it, despite her expressed desire to do so.

There was nothing I could do to help her until she decided that it was safe to let go of the hurt and disappointment surrounding the loss of the relationship. The vulnerability she felt from the situation stayed with her, and it did not feel safe to release it for fear of opening herself once again to heartache. This stuck energy resides in the emotional energy body, and her unwillingness to release it keeps it there, blocking any new relationship from coming in. When you feel threatened, your heart chakra (chest area) closes. It feels as though you are cut off from others. It is a sense of vulnerability, and feeing vulnerable closes you off to abundance. Opening your heart can be painful or exhilarating. When you open your heart to someone, you get a blast of energy that can take you to the depths of sorrow or soaring through the clouds. Be careful when and with whom you choose to open your heart. Use your newfound energetic awareness in determining if the person is energetically aligned with you and whether the relationship would be for the highest good.

From these two cases, you can see that you have ultimate control over whether to hold onto stuck energy or to release it.

You can tell when a chakra is blocked by using a pendulum. Have the person lie down to test the body chakras or sit to evaluate the crown chakra. Hold the pendulum over the chakra. If it is blocked, the pendulum will remain still or sway from side to side or back and forth.

If it is open, it will move in a circle over the area. The bigger the circle and the faster it moves, the more open the chakra.

The stuck energy can also be felt as a density or thickening of the energy. Those who are stuck in many aspects of their lives have a generalized heaviness about them. You can sense it in their slow movements, in their lack of abundance, and in their resistance to most suggestions (I call this the "Yeah, but…" Consistency). There may also be a lack of motivation to change what holds them back. They tend to be closed overall and very little can be done from the outside to intervene. They must decide to make the change for themselves, so do not waste your energy trying to convince them otherwise. Their energy is very close to the body, so they appear dull when encountering them, as opposed to those who are inspired and fulfilled feeling bright and radiating with energy.

Once you have pinpointed the blocked area, focus on it when you do the energetic dumping exercise to release it from your body, send white light to the area to clear it, or address it directly with Reiki or other form of energy healing. A Reiki practitioner can help remove the block, but only if you are willing to release it. No one can force it out. Or you can close your eyes and concentrate on the spot, asking what is causing it and why you are choosing to keep it. When you are ready, imagine it turning into vapor and gently release it from your body.

If it is stuck in the emotional or mental body, you will go through the same process. To open, you need to feel safe with a strong willingness to let go. Performing the grounding and protection exercises can help with this, along with trusting yourself and the guidance you receive.

Once opened, you will experience the world much differently. Opening the chakras to the energy of others results in an intense sensation of whatever the person is experiencing. It is especially difficult opening to those in intense mental, physical, or emotional pain. This is why regularly using the protection methods we discussed is so important.

During my Reiki training, I went through a process called *attunement*, wherein my palms were opened to enable me to give energy to others. There were unexpected reactions to this process. Once I was attuned, everything felt different; things were more sensitive to the touch, and I was acutely aware of the way energy was moving around me. I even had different reactions to foods and alcohol.

After my first attunement, a glass of wine made me sick to my stomach. I also saw energy flowing through tarot cards as I read them. After the second attunement, by body seemed to be more acclimated to the new vibrational level, and I could take my energy and travel in my energy body. After the third, my sensitivity to the energies of others was more accurate than ever before. I could see textures and densities around people. I can open and close my chakras at will; open when I am in a session, alone, or with friends, and closed when I am out in public.

Attunement is one way to open; knowledge is another way to open to different energies. Knowledge from books, lectures, and experiences help you move your energy and open it in ways never possible prior to gaining new insights. In this way, you can open yourself to the energies of new cultures, new beliefs, new ways of thinking, and ultimately, new ways of looking at yourself.

With each bit of stuck energy that is released, a layer is peeled back and the next layer is revealed. In this way, a gradual unfoldment takes place. You think you have addressed an issue and another one pops up. This is because the layer that had been blocking the next in line to be addressed was removed, so that it could be unveiled. It is the process of self-discovery and allows the opportunity to address lessons in bite-sized pieces. With each lesson learned, a greater opening is possible.

Techniques for Drawing Energy

Whether you are aware of it or not, you are actively drawing energy to yourself. We attract what we are inside. Every thought, feeling, belief, and action draws certain types of energy to you. The key is to be intentional with the type of energy you are pulling. The active approach to drawing energy requires paying attention to what is around you and being discriminating in your choices. Everything you choose to wear, own, think, say, feel, and participate in carries particular energy. Be careful of what you say, for you draw it to you. "I will never find another job," "I will never find the right relation-ship," or countless other negative statements will get you exactly what you are announcing. "I don't want to fail" sends out the message of failure. "I hate being picked on" invites bullies. "I'm so worried about bankruptcy" leads to business failure. Take stock in what you say and think, for that is what you will draw to you.

Depending on what you want to draw to yourself, whether it is a relationship, a job, or a way of being, you must begin by visualizing what you are trying to attract. The type of energy you are set-up to draw to yourself, even if it conflicts with what you say you want, manifests in concrete ways. Take relationships, for example.

Many people try to attract the right relationship, yet face repeated disappointment. Does the idea of a "healthy relationship" seem foreign to you? Is it even possible to have a healthy relationship? What would it look like and what would you feel like to be with the right person? Many people experience the pattern of being in the same type of relationship over and over—but with different partners. The faces change, but the basic type of relationship is the same. Certain themes may pervade the interaction: possessiveness/jealousy, lack of commitment, the need to control—all aspects of attracting a person who lacks self-esteem and confidence. This exemplifies drawing the wrong type of energy in the form of the relationships in your life.

What it is about your thoughts and beliefs regarding your Self that draws, say, a controlling or jealous type of person? It could be that you feel unable to make decisions for yourself or believe that if the person really loves you, they will be jealous of others that are around you.

Ask yourself what you want in a relationship and in your life. Are there specific things you would like to experience in a relationship that you have never gotten from your past interactions? What are you looking for? Exclude considerations like appearance and occupation, but focus on how that person treats you and makes you feel. Are you looking for a companion to share common interests? Do you prefer a relationship where you both have your own interests, yet come together to share what you experience individually? How much freedom are you looking for and how much freedom are you willing to allow?

The truth is that the relationship you are in mirrors how you feel about yourself and the type of energy you project. It may be that you, too, have low self-esteem and require an objective look at what draws this type of person to you. The way you feel about yourself on the inside can be felt by others. When you like yourself and have self-confidence, others will enjoy being around you more and you will attract confident, happy people. The more optimistic you are about yourself and about life in general, the more likely you are to attract others who are optimistic as well.

It all starts with self-exploration and the journey of appreciating yourself for who you are. If you are not sure who you are, all the more reason to discover your core identity. By understanding yourself, you will be in a better position to determine what you want in your life. Find your passion and pursue your interests. People like to be around those who have something they love doing. It also allows you to express yourself in ways that connect you with others who may have similar interests. Learn to communicate your interests in a way that engages others, as well as listening intently to what they have to say.

Uncover your unique and special qualities. Appreciate yourself for the wonderful aspects you bring to a relationship. Then the energy you project and what you attract, in relationships and in all aspects of your life, will be aligned with who you are, how you feel about yourself, and what you want.

To draw sufficient energy to accomplish your goals, you must be sufficiently motivated and possess the desire to attract or accomplish your goals. If you merely say you want something, but do not feel strongly about it, then insufficient energy will be drawn to support your desire. If you require additional incentive, use pictures of what you are trying to draw to you. This is the purpose of a vision board: to align yourself with the energies you are trying to draw to you. You can also make a list of how your life would be improved if you attain your desire.

Flowing With Natural Cycles

There are particular energies associated with natural cycles and natural objects. It is valuable to understand the natural rhythm of life and the patterns that create your personal cycles and to be in harmony with them. There are times when it is essential to rest and other times when it is important to push forward. Increase your awareness of these natural trends and allow yourself to flow with them rather than resist them. Internal cycles are present as well, with hormonal cycles changing daily and monthly. Astrological cycles can enhance or diminish your energy and motivation. They may incline you toward a specific goal or desire. People out of step with these cycles or who are unaware of them experience a sense of disconnect with the energy around them.

Moving in rhythm with the natural cycles around us and within us is essential for vibrational discernment. Moon cycles and seasons are two examples. There are many stories about how the full moon affects behavior and mood. One of my clients was telling me how she had the urge to purge and reorganize her home. She gets motivated to do this periodically, so we tracked her activity. It turns out that her purging always takes place during the waning moon; a time symbolic of cleansing and banishing.

Here are the moon phases and their associated energies to use in tracking your own personal cycles:

- **New Moon** (1st quarter)—New projects/new beginnings (first 3 days are dark)
- **Waxing** (2nd quarter)—Gives a boost of power or to grow or develop a project or idea
- **Full** (3rd quarter)—Maximum power for manifestation, culmination of plans, and projects close to fruition
- **Waning** (4th quarter)—Used to banish or remove (bad habits, negative energies/people, lose weight, etc.), reorganize, purge, and plan for the next New Moon. Also good for study and meditation.
- **Lunar Eclipse**—Used to eliminate things you no longer want in your life (health issue, bills, a physical aspect of yourself, etc.)
- **Blue Moon**—Use these energies to set intentions for the next two years (Blue Moon energy). When it coincides with a Lunar Eclipse, use to release and banish things you no longer want in your life.

Seasons are another powerful time and each may affect you in certain ways. Seasonal Affective Disorder is one type of depression directly connected to the seasons. Most of those suffering from this experience depression, very low energy, and moodiness starting in the autumn months when the days grow dark earlier and the effect can last through the winter. Less often, people have this reaction in the spring and early summer. Having mood swings or getting urges to do things seemingly for no reason have a high likelihood of being connected to these internal and external cycles.

The energies associated with the seasons are:

Autumn ("Prepare") Autumn is a time for harvest and preparing for the winter ahead. It is a time to move toward new opportunities and is the best time to initiate change. Shed the past, the outmoded, and whatever is no longer appropriate to your path. Plan for the future. Plant seeds for what you want to come into your life, knowing that they will grow and be ready for harvest by the following autumn.

Spring ("New Beginnings") Spring is a time to once again become active and to tap into the energy of new life. It is a time of growth and resurrection, rebirth, and the promise of a fresh start. It is a good time to initiate efforts toward your goals.

Summer ("Fulfillment") Summer is a time when seeds have burst into blossom, fruit ripens, and life grows. Plantings from the previous autumn come to fruition, and a sense of fulfillment is in the air. It is a good time for personal development and strengthening resolve toward your desires.

Winter ("Withdraw") Winter is a time when supplies are low, plants and trees are dormant, and animals conserve their energy. It is a time of death and withdrawal. Winter is the season to go within and listen to your higher self. A time of meditation and inactivity is best used to allow internal changes to take place.

Exercise 6-3: Track Your Personal Cycles

Keep a journal of your energy highs and lows. Record the date, the moon phase (new, waxing, full, and waning), the season of the year, and your energy level on a scale of 1 (low) to 10 (high). Identify patterns in your energy levels and notice correlations between your energy and the moon phase or season. When are you most likely to have lots of energy? When do you feel most like resting?

Natural Energies

Every aspect of nature has its own energies. Animals, plants, and minerals all contain various actual and metaphysical qualities that can be felt and used to draw particular energies. Whole books have been written about stones, trees, and other aspects of nature. For the purposes of this text, here is a small sample of the energies represented by minerals and trees.

Minerals

Amethyst ("Awareness") Protection, purification, divine connection, dreams, overcoming addictions, healing, psychic opening, mental clarity, peace of mind, intuition

Aventurine ("Luck") Money, gambling, health, creativity, courage, leadership, decision-making

Citrine ("Manifestation") Anti-nightmare, protection, personal will, mental clarity, creativity, dreams, success, prosperity, manifest personal power, initiative, endurance

Clear Quartz ("Amplification") Clearing, cleansing, enhancement, attain goals, direct and transmit energy

Hematite ("Challenge") Grounding, making the spiritual physical, self-control, balance, focus, clarity

Rose Quartz ("Love") Gentleness, emotional healing, release of stress, peace, comfort, companionship

Sodalite ("Communication") Intuition, enhanced insight, meditation, wisdom, direction of purpose, self-esteem, self-trust, trust in others, ability to verbalize true feelings

Trees

Trees have some of the most powerful energies on the planet. It is possible to derive great benefit from interacting with trees. Here are some examples:

Cedar ("Protection") Cleansing, purification, strengthening and enhancement of inner potential, healing, renewal, banishing

Maple ("Creativity") Promises, inspiration, balance of masculine and feminine energies, love, abundance, attraction, communication

Oak ("Strength") Endurance, open doorways to inner realms, fruitful labor, power, courage, abundance, authority, money, health, fertility, masculine energies

Pine ("Cleansing") Protection, balance emotions, eliminate guilt, increased psychic sensitivity, creative expression, immortality, purification

Poplar ("Manifestation") Time to pursue your dreams and projects, great rewards, quick result, opportunity, broad possibilities, strong foundation, overcome fear and self-doubt, endure hardship, time to manifest, success, recognition, fame

Sycamore ("Gifts") New life, express prior knowledge in new ways, intuitive messages, help and support comes in abundance

Willow ("Intuition") Inspiration, dreams, divination, flexibility, messages, feminine energies, magic, death

Colors

Colors also carry with them particular energies. They have very specific frequencies on the visible electromagnetic spectrum, with red at the lower frequency up to purple with the highest frequency. There are volumes written about the psychology of color and how they promote a sense of well being, increase hunger, soothe or agitate, or even promote a sense of trust. The colors you wear have much to do with how people react to you. The selection of what to wear can be directly related to your mood or even your vibrational frequency. Ever take something out of your closet, put it on, and it just does not look or feel right? So you select another garment and that one feels much better? It increases your confidence and raises your spirits. When it feels good to you, it is likely aligned with your auric energy for that day. At the same time, you may choose clothing based on the image you want to project. Black can project power; blue can elicit trust; white is the color of purity and cleanliness, e.g., police uniforms are blue, physician lab coats are white. Specific color energies can also be drawn using candles. Here is a brief overview of the effect color can have.

- **Black** ("Protection") Ward negativity, remove hexes, power, focus
- **Blue** ("Tranquility") Dreams, meditation, intuition, understanding, faithfulness, change
- **Green** ("Luck") Fertility, healing, prosperity, changing directions, courage
- **Purple** ("Wisdom") Power, spirit, self-assurance, influence, intuition, progress
- **Red** ("Passion") Strength, energy, vigor, sexuality, confidence, power, energy, driving force
- **White** ("Purity") Protection, truth, sincerity, justice, ward doubt/fear
- **Yellow** ("Intellect") Mental alertness, learning, creativity, joy

Grouping objects of like energy intensifies the effect. For example, if you wish to draw money to energy, write down your desire and store it in a box lined with green fabric and containing coins, aventurine, and other personal symbols of money, wealth, and abundance. The strategy of grouping items amplifies the energy through using objects of a similar energy pattern. In this way, the objects will create an energy transfer one to the other and intensify the vibrational pattern's effect on the space. There are times you may want to amplify a particular vibration or minimize it, so be aware of how objects are grouped in your home and office.

Charging Objects

Any number of items may be charged to draw energy for your special purpose. Clothing, jewelry, and miscellaneous objects are all appropriate to use as talismans. To identify an object you wish to charge, begin by sensing the energy of the things you wear and carry. Do you attribute a special vibration to any of them? Is there a new object you would like to turn into a protective amulet? Is there an antique of some sort that you would like to select for your purpose? In making your selection, consider the energy it will take to intensify its charge. It will take less energy on your part to charge an object that has been with you the longest or the most consistently; it has been absorbing your vibrational pattern over time. Both new objects and antique (formerly owned by someone other than you) need to first be cleared of the vibrations of everything it has come in contact with. The challenge with the old object is in clearing it of any malevolent energy, while maintaining any positive vibrations that have been imprinted on the item. In the case of the brand new object, it can be easier to charge with a specific purpose or desire, yet it is difficult to determine how much energy the object will need to absorb for it to be effective.

To charge an object with specific intent, hold it in your most energetically tuned hand, that is, whichever hand projects the strongest energy. Close your eyes and concentrate on the desire you have for the object. For example, if you want to imprint a green candle to have the energies of bringing money to you, hold the candle and picture money falling from the sky and surrounding you, envision providing wonderful service in exchange for the money, and smile as you see your wealth grow in your mind's eye. Ask for the specific amount of money you require. Always ask for your desires to manifest with harm to none. Afterward, light the candle to release the money energy.

The same process is performed with any object. Be clear with your intent and your request as you hold the object. Phrase your intent in present tense, as though it was already true, such as "This object bears the vibration of success, prosperity, and abundance for all of my endeavors, with harm to none." It is best to imprint objects with positive affirmations and always with harm to none. Remember, whatever energy you put out into the Universe comes back to you threefold.

Directing Energy

Many cultures have methods of moving and directing energy. It is important that your energetic awareness include the types of techniques and beliefs that resonate most closely with your vibrational patterns. Understand that with each shift, the techniques you employ and the beliefs you hold will change. Flexibility is one of the most important aspects of energy, since change is inevitable and resistance to change creates discord within and without you. To empower yourself fully and increase your effectiveness, I recommend taking aspects of all systems that speak to you, combining them, and adding your personal touch to the mix.

Direct cause and effect are nonexistent when dealing at the sub-atomic level of energy; rather, there is a state of influence and potentiality. Many potential outcomes exist simultaneously until we decide on the one we want. In most cases, many variables move the energy to the final outcome, and not all of them can be accounted for or directly influenced. Basic cause and effect applies to the mundane actions one can take, such as you tug on a weed (cause) and it comes out of the ground (effect); here you can see a direct line from one to the other. With energetic actions, there is a continuous state of shifting, no single interaction leading directly to the next. Your thoughts and intentions send energy moving in a certain direction, and as they shift and change, so does their effect on the outcome.

Also simultaneous, apparently unconnected occurrences contribute to an outcome. The Universe makes adjustments as needed, that we may or may not be aware of. We are not able to take into account everything that may happen or that could affect what we wish for ourselves. Our requests to the Universe, as well as our thoughts and actions, shift energy to enhance or detract from the desired outcome.

There is a constant redistribution of energetic possibilities due to the perpetual bombardment of thoughts, feelings, and actions upon the Universal Energy. Opening to these energetic shifts allows choices based on the most up-to-date energy patterns. Getting in synch with that which is around us, whether it emanates from people, places, objects, or ourselves, is to experience the wavelength of the situation and understand its true nature. The guidance system we use to make these choices must include an understanding of the energies within and around us.

Intention

There must be clear intent before energy can be moved in a specific direction. The desire and motivation of the originator directs the flow and texture of the energy. What manifests is dictated by intention.

Intention is the key to focusing your attention and, thereby, directing the energy.

Energy is directed by determining a specific goal and visualizing the attainment of that goal. The moving of the energy is what is important; the ability to direct the energy to manifest what intention and will dictates. When you formulate your desires, be clear in what you want, and your motivation for it. If you do not know what you want, you cannot direct your energy toward it. Making the choice, understanding why you are choosing it, and tapping into the motivation behind it serves to direct energy in a laser-focused way. The accumulation and specific release of energy is the key to manifestation of a vision.

Get Permission

Before getting into the best way to direct energy (I advise against sending out negative or condemning energies—whatever you put out comes back threefold), let us talk about ethics. Unless you have the person's permission, you are interfering with their path, their growth, and their lessons. To ethically direct energy, do not administer healing or intervene in any way without the express permission of the person receiving the energy.

How can wanting something positive for someone cause any ethical concerns? It does if you are going against the will of another. Here are three examples. You may want a sick person to get well, but this person may want to die, or enjoy the attention the illness attracts. Wanting someone to quit smoking and become healthy may go against the smoker's desire to gain certain benefits from the habit. You may wish for your brother to change to a more profitable line of work, but his values could place quality of life above financial reward. When you ask for something involving someone else without permission, you are going against the will of another. You may be asking for something that they do not want for themselves.

Each of us has free will to make choices in any way we deem fit for whatever reasons, obvious or obscured, and it is not up to someone else to judge our decisions or go against our wishes. This creates energy that is forceful, dense, and evil. Evil? In the context of prayer? Yes, absolutely. It is immoral and manipulative to go against the will of another, no matter what form it takes or what your reasons are.

Sending energy of any kind, even in the form of light and love, requires permission and specificity as to its ultimate purpose. Your idea about what is best for them needs to align with what they envision for themselves. Acting in the highest good of someone else requires that you have their permission to assist them in manifesting a certain condition in their life.

Ask permission before sending healing, prayers, or any other form of "asking" for someone else's benefit. Even when you feel that the person is heading down a path of self-destruction, do not intervene without permission. I have seen people "asking" for others to change their beliefs, see things the way they think would be "best" for them, and essentially, trying to control the way they handle their lives. This is ultimately a judgment against them, that they do not know what is best for their own lives. If you believe that all energy is connected, then it is also an assumption that you know how their challenge plays a role in the greater scheme of the Universe.

Experiences of all kinds offer us the opportunity to learn lessons and understand the energies associated with certain choices. The challenges faced in life are there to teach us and to strengthen us as we overcome adversity. It is up to us whether we choose to grow or not. Whenever you pray for someone else or wish something for them that you feel is in their best interest, understand that you are inserting yourself into their karmic path and could potentially deny them valuable lessons they need to learn. This includes illness, financial issues, emotional strain, anxiety, and any other challenges you can think of. Each person must have the opportunity to move through these challenges in their own way and in their own time. If that obstacle is removed before it has served its purpose, then we must repeat certain situations in order to finally get the lessons we are meant to have in this lifetime.

Understanding your own path and what is in your own best interest is challenging enough; to determine what is best for another is unethical and impractical. Focus on what you want for yourself and get permission to energetically intervene for others.

Prayer or Blessing

Prayers are testaments to a specific intention; a way of connecting to Source and directing your energy through applying your will. Prayer is an effective way to direct energy. It is a form of setting an intention using carefully chosen words and then pairing them with a heartfelt request while connecting to Source. When you concentrate on what you are saying and asking for within the prayer, as opposed to saying it by rote, this is a powerful method to use.

Prayers and blessings are designed for particular purposes. There are prayers for guidance, purpose, balance, gratitude, inner peace, protection, etc. They can be traditional prayers, modern prayer versions, or a prayer that you write yourself. Generally, it is a request to Source that a particular condition comes to fruition. In its highest form, prayer is a way of giving thanks and sending out the energy of gratitude for all that is in your life.

The energy of prayer and the power we have to bless or condemn is as effective for lay people as for those who are officially ordained. It all comes down to the connection we feel with the sentiment and with the Divine that creates a connection that ultimately serves the intention of the prayer.

Here are the general guidelines for directing energy through blessings/prayers.

Framing the blessing: When writing the prayer yourself or at the end of a pre-written blessing, include the phrase, *for the highest good,* or *the highest good of all,* or *for my highest good and the highest good of those around me.* Most traditional prayers end with saying, "Amen," meaning "so be it," yet that does not set the energy of having it occur in the best interest of all concerned, simply that you wish it to be so.

Throughout the blessing, frame the intention in a way that is best for all, in the highest good of all, and the desire will come in the best possible way...or not. This way of *asking* is also a protection, so that if what you ask for is not in your best interest (there may be something better, or what you want could be changing in the near future due to some other unforeseeable event), then it will not occur. It addresses the old phrase *be careful what you wish for.*

Include the phrase, "With harm to none." This is important, because there is a series of events that energetically come together in order for whatever you asked for to come to fruition. If you ask for money without the *harm to none* intention, it could be that you acquire the money through the death of a loved one and a subsequent inheritance.

Phrasing the blessing: When writing your own blessing, first decide what you want the focus or intention of the blessing to be. What is your motivation for wanting this particular condition in your life? Think about its implications and whether or not it may be manipulative in any way. In the case of a blessing for a romantic relationship, a manipulative request would be asking that a particular person that you designate be attracted to you as opposed to asking that the right person come into your life.

Write the phrases of the blessing in present tense, such as "The right person is in my life," rather than "The right person will enter my life." Say it as though it already happened. Let your words own what you want. It is waiting for you to claim what is yours.

Ask for *what* you want and not the *how* of what you want. Asking for the money to buy a house is determining how the house will manifest. Asking for the house itself and letting the energies find the best way to do that opens a much greater realm of possibilities as to how it could come about. Many times it is not in a way that you would have thought of. A friend of mine who had no money acquired a business she always wanted in a most unexpected way...the owner gave her the store and said she would be back in a year to receive payment and complete the sale. All went well; she paid the former owner and successfully owned and ran the store for ten years. That was an option that never occurred to her; she was looking at getting the money in order to get the business. Our experiences limit our vision of what is possible; allow the Universe to determine the best way to deliver your request.

Some like to write blessings with a rhyming pattern as in a poem. Others prefer a free style phrase. Go with whatever you feel best directs the energy and feels right to you. I do recommend writing the blessing in short lines to focus the energy as precisely as possible.

Pull in correspondences within the phrasing that support the energy of your intention. Use the stones, colors, trees, or elements mentioned earlier in this chapter, or any others you may want to include, such as angelic energies.

Exercise 6-4: Write a Blessing

Write a blessing for yourself using the guidelines in this section. After ensuring that what you have written is ethical and carries with it the proper energies to support your desire, ground and protect yourself, and then say the blessing out loud. Compare how you feel before and after you say the blessing.

Reiki Directing Energy

One method to enhance the ability to observe and direct energy is through the practice of Reiki (pronounced ray-key), meaning Universal Life Force. Reiki is a system of natural healing that channels energy from the Universe into the practitioner and out through the hands. Ultimately, it is a technique for moving energy through the body of the practitioner. There are around 200 forms of Reiki, ranging from rattles used by Shamans to the hands-on techniques of the Usui practitioner. Of late, the training has been watered down so as to be less effective, with courses like "Become a powerful Reiki master in 48 hours." You cannot become a powerful anything in 48 hours. It takes practice, clearing of the self, self mastery, and a connection to Spirit.

Reiki is a gentle yet powerful form of hands-on healing that is effective in the treatment of stress, anxiety, and pain. Reiki is best when used as part of a holistic approach to health, which includes mind, body, emotions, and spirit, as well as traditional medical intervention when needed. Reiki is not a replacement for regular medical treatment by a licensed physician. A Reiki practitioner can balance the energy centers of the body, or chakras, to maximize the flow of Source Energy or chi (ki) through the body, affording increased health and immune system functionality. Strengthening the flow of chi is essential to physical, mental, emotional, and spiritual well-being.

The practice of Reiki requires intention to direct healing energy to the recipient. Reiki training teaches how to move energy in specific ways and directing energy for a specific purpose. This method is applied to healing, calming, or balancing someone, someplace, or some situation.

The practitioner is attuned at three progressively higher levels. An attunement is the act of opening someone and bringing this person into harmony with Universal Light Force to make it possible to channel energy. In Reiki, the student is attuned to particular symbols representative of energies used to heal and direct energy. With each level, more advanced techniques are revealed to the student. For students, make sure that the classes include lessons on grounding and protection and that you are attuned before practicing on others. If not, you are giving the subject your own energy rather than channeling Universal Life Force, and this is likely to result in extreme fatigue and/or illness. It is best to take the levels at least six months to one year apart, in order to assimilate the information and to master the skills at each level. Like mastery of any technique, it takes many, many hours of study and practice.

In the practice of Reiki, both the recipient and the practitioner must actively participate in order to create a shift within the subject. The energy must flow between the participants to be effective. Important elements for this exchange include having an open mind and a positive intent displayed by both the practitioner and the subject.

The subject must grant permission in order to receive Reiki energy. The release of undesirable vibrations from the client is dependent upon the client's willingness to let them go. The practitioner cannot force out the problem or force the energy in; however, the energy administered can loosen the problem's grip to make it easier for the client to release it.

Negative energy is accumulated by physical pain, psychic pain, or emotional pain. The ability to release it is proportionate to the amount of fear the person has around letting go of the issue. Those who are afraid to live without the familiar feeling, regardless of its negative effect, will not be likely to release it during a Reiki session, regardless of the skill of the practitioner.

Willingness to open is essential in the healing process. A space must be created in the recipient's energy field in order to accept positive energy. Reiki sessions are energizing for both practitioner and subject when the person is receptive to the energy and open to the effects, because the energy flows freely.

Learning to perform Reiki is one path toward heightened energetic awareness and an effective technique to direct energy.

For additional reading on Reiki, some good resources include *Hands of Light* by Barbara Ann Brennan and *Pranic Healing* by Choa Kok Sui.

Thought and Vision

Energy can be directed using an intentional thought and envisioning the designated target. In this way, you can direct energy toward yourself, someone else (again, always with their permission), or even toward a situation. You can direct energy to have an effect in the present or send it into the future to affect a particular circumstance, as when you know you will need an energy boost, for example, during an interview or presentation.

When you want to foster a comfortable environment in which to deliver a presentation, arrive early and stand in front of the room. Plant your feet on the floor and envision your energy touching every corner of the space while intending that your presentation be delivered in the best possible way for the highest good of those in attendance. Feel your presence fill the room. Be comfortable in the space. Beam your intention wall to wall or if outdoors, create an imaginary boundary in which to contain the energy. Take a deep breath and release it. Go on with confidence!

When using this technique for a future circumstance, sit in a quiet place where you will not be disturbed. Close your eyes and set the date you wish to affect in your mind. Picture yourself in the situation at the location where the appointment will take place. Send energy to yourself in the form of the anticipated need. Say you are sending the energy to scheduled job interview happening in the near future. You tend to get nervous and forget what you wanted to say during interviews, so send yourself calming energy containing the intention of remembering the important points you want to make. Craft this in a way that speaks to your particular need for the situation. Always send the energy to yourself, not to the interviewer.

Use this technique to adjust and balance the energy for harmonious and positive interactions.

Using Tools to Direct Energy

In every movie you have ever seen where a wizard is present, there is also a wand to help him direct his magic. A wand is an extension of your body and should be cut the length from your elbow to your forefinger. It is a physical representation of your intention. It directs your passion and intent. The wand is the tool of the Fire element that sparks your motivation and your energy. The type of wood that is used can support the intention you are trying to put forth. Check out the tree energies listed earlier to see if any of them coincide with your intentions. I suggest harvesting branches already shed to create your wand. Some believe that the best material to make a wand is copper for its conducting powers.

In the same way as a wand can direct energy, any tool you are using for a particular purpose acts in the same way. A painter's brush is the tool which directs the energy, taking his imagination and bringing it into the physical by way of the brush through the medium of paint. A fencer uses a foil to direct energy toward the opponent with the intention of victory. A programmer uses coding as his tool of choice. A writer uses a keyboard or pen to direct his thoughts and energies onto the page. A gardener uses various tools to direct her energy and produce a magnificent garden that started as an idea in her mind.

Exercise 6-5: Energetic Tools

> What is your tool of choice and how does it help you direct your energies?

Force of Will

Energy can be directed through force of will. This requires focused attention toward the object or condition you want coupled with intense desire. See the end result with crystal clarity. This is the force by which astounding feats are accomplished, such as finishing a marathon despite intense physical challenges. You see the end result, you want it desperately, and you apply the strength of your will to achieve it. It helps you to laser-focus your energy and direct it toward the aspiration.

With any of these methods, it is important to gather your energy and focus it by whatever means that works best for you. Scattered energy cannot be directed, so get rid of the distractions, the doubts, and the negative thoughts so you can use your energy in the most effective way possible.

Chapter 7 – Manifesting & Energy

Removing Blocks to Manifesting

Would you like to manifest more money, a new home, your ideal career? So many people have tried Law of Attraction methods, created vision boards, said daily affirmations, and thought about what they want in attempts to manifest their desires—with no result. All of that time wasted, hoping that the desired result would soon happen. You have probably heard that if you follow your passion, the money will come. Yet it still has not appeared. Let us take a look at the barriers to manifesting and how to overcome them.

Before you can direct energy toward creating your best life, you need to understand the mindset that stops you from doing so. Some common energetic road blocks that obstruct your ability to manifest your desires include:

- Fear of rejection—Worrying that if you make changes and go for it, those closest to you will no longer consider you part of the group/family/circle of friends

- Desire for acceptance—When you do something that is the basis for you to be accepted by a person or group of people so you can fit in

- Wanting to please someone else—This happens when someone close to you has expectations of you, and these have nothing to do with what you want for yourself

- Uncertainty of what you really want—If you do not know what you really want, then you cannot set goals or envision your life any differently than it is right now

- You are unclear about who you truly are—You cannot settle on what you want, because nothing feels right to you. This is a result of having done things to please others for so long that you are not sure who you are and what you need

- You lack self-confidence—You do not trust that you have what it takes to get what you want or you do not trust that you can possibly know what is best for you
- You do not believe you deserve to be happy—A large part of this stems from your definition of happiness. What would it take to make you truly happy and to feel fulfilled?
- You do not believe it is possible to get what you want—The vision you have for yourself seems too lofty; after all, others have told you to *be realistic*, so they must be right and you opt for the acceptable and mundane. Not so! You cannot see past what is currently in your life to make the leap into your ideal life
- Your vision is not really your ideal life—The vision you have is a slight modification of how you are living now rather than a clear picture of your truly idyllic life

Throughout my life, the things that I have focused on manifested. When I see the outcome clearly, the desired result transpires. I do not dictate how it happens, I just determine the *what* and have no doubt that it will happen. With every fiber of my being, my desire is aligned with the vision, which is aligned with divine energy. I know that it has already happened and will come into being in its own time and in its own way. I become excited knowing it is waiting to transpire. My feeling is associated with the outcome.

One instance of manifestation is when I wanted to move into a particular house. As I walked through, I saw new color on the walls, my furniture placed perfectly in the space, the calm and inspiring energy I imprinted there, and the happiness I would experience living there. Then I took action. It needed a complete renovation, which I undertook and completed in six weeks. My furniture was moved in and fit exactly where I had imagined it would go. The final product was the precise image I had envisioned so clearly in my mind's eye. This is a good example of how simply wishing and envisioning is not enough; action must be taken toward your desire.

An illustration of the old adage "Be careful what you wish for" occurred when I *asked* the Universe to give me time to write. I then got laryngitis and lost my voice... for eight months! It gave me plenty of time to write, since I could not vocally interact with my friends, family, or colleagues, so all communication was done by writing. During that time, I finished writing my first novel and realized that the way that I asked for what I wanted was not specific enough and did not contain the specification "With harm to none," including to myself. Despite the lingering challenge, my voice strength is now an indicator that whenever I feel throat discomfort or my voice starting to go, it is time to stop talking and focus on writing.

So how can you make this work for you? Shift the energy around these self-limiting beliefs with these strategies:

1. **Doubt, fear, and worry**—These toxic states of being block the flow of energy; when you know who you are and what you are here to do, the fear goes away. Stop the negative self-talk and the negative things about yourself that you tell others—I am in so much debt, I have no energy, My life is a mess.—What you say is what you pull into your life. Also, stop doubting your vision; it prevents anything from happening.

2. **The "How"**—do not worry about the how and when, just know what you want and why. The why, for example, could be that you want a better place to live; this is what you need the money for. So rather than focusing on the money, focus on a new place to live—ask for your right residence, where you can feel happy, peaceful, and inspired, or whatever it is you would like—and let the Universe figure out the best way to make it happen.

3. **We are not separate**—we are connected to everything and everyone. We create using the power of 2—you and Source energy—we co-create with the universe in accordance with our life purpose. We use the guidance of Divine Will and apply personal will to carry it through. The vibrational patterns you express in the physical realm are duplicated on the spiritual plane; adjust the pattern to one more conducive with what you want to manifest.

4. **Thoughts carry tangible energy**. Everything you experience is a reflection of your thoughts and beliefs. Doubt is created when the more you think about something you want, the more it evades you. Use a thought to seed what you want and then let go of your attachment to it. That means that you trust the universe and are okay with whatever happens. You are detached from the outcome.

5. **The Law of Attraction** is for pulling in like energies that can lead to manifesting your desires. It is a way of setting up energy patterns with the intention of matching the vibration of what you want to make available for yourself. These patterns of projected energy reflect what

you are, so stay conscious of the level at which you are vibrating. Be aware of the energy you are setting up, for this can work to your benefit, as well as to your detriment. You can create an energy pattern that pulls particular opportunities toward you. When you take the right action, this then enables you to achieve your desire. At the same time, when you believe that you lack money, an energetic pattern of deficiency is created and lack is what you will attract. This is called poverty consciousness.

6. **Source** is the overarching energy and all else is subordinate to it. We cannot tell the Universe what, when, and how we want things done; we can, however, influence and open the energy toward our desires. We can benefit from Source's omnipresent knowing. Tap into Divine will, and ask for that which is in your highest good. Ask to be shown the way. Think about a time when you did not follow your intuition (a form of Divine guidance) and things did not work out for the best. Now think about a time when you did follow your intuition; I bet everything went smoothly. Your intuition is the Universe speaking through your higher self into the conscious mind. Intuitive messages *feel* different than regular, impulsive thoughts do. You will learn more about differentiating between them in Chapter 8.

7. **Affirmations** that are not aligned with your energy will not work. They are used to speak to your subconscious mind, which is where we manifest—not in the conscious mind—and to set-up energy patterns. Affirmations need to be formulated in trust and knowing that what you want is waiting to transpire. Use the following guidelines to create powerful affirmations that point to the outcome you desire.

Let us begin by considering the following statement: "I will pay off my debt, so that I no longer have to worry and struggle."

Instead try: "I am joyously living in financial abundance; all my needs are met." Feel the difference?

- Use the present tense. State your affirmation in the present tense, formulating the statement in a way that says the desired condition is already true.

- Focus on what you want...not what you do not want. The sentence above focuses on debt, the exact thing you do not want. The modified sentence puts the focus directly on what you do want, financial abundance.

- Keep it simple. Use brief, pointed statements that get to the heart of what you are asking for.

- Include your vision and how it makes you feel. Include how you see yourself living or being when your desire manifests. Say something like, "I am happily entertaining my friends in my dream home."

When you hit upon the affirmation that leads to manifestation, your heart chakra (energy center) opens up, a smile bursts onto your face, and you feel that it is indeed possible to have what you desire.

So, to overcome blocks, know who you are and why you are here, allow the universal energy to determine the how, let go of attachment, formulate an effective affirmation, and know that what you want is already here.

Define Your Desires

Choosing what you are asking for is a critical step. What drives your choices? Do you make choices out of guilt or fear of judgment? Do you determine what you want based solely on whether or not you have the money or will be able to earn the money? While this is an important consideration, think of the lifestyle you desire rather than focusing on having a lot of money. How much do you actually need to live a happy life?

Some people make decisions based on the need to go along with traditional, societal expectations of what defines success and happiness. Some allow the opinions of others to determine what is best. Do you sway to their jealousy or their reservations? Do you lack confidence and simply figure that everyone else must be right and knows what is best for you? "Jim is really smart, so I should listen to his advice rather than exploring my own ideas." Stop worrying about what everybody else thinks; it is time to define your own wants and needs. Their advice is based on their own experiences and understanding. What they do and what they believe can be taken into consideration, while you determine what feels right for you. You have a unique path, so do the research, envision how your choices will affect your life, and build the energy behind your goal.

When you make choices based on what others want from you, or what they believe is right, you will never be happy nor come fully into yourself, and may likely have regrets for not following your dreams. When you give in to negative thoughts like, "It cannot be done," or give in to someone else's negativity, you zap your power and take a step backward in your spiritual growth.

As we have discussed, distancing yourself from negative people or situations that drain you of your enthusiasm will get rid of doubt and enable you to see what is possible. Trusting that you know what is best for yourself, and that your dreams were put into your head for a reason, is the most important part of this. Trust that you have what it takes to get what you want, and draw on your personal power. If you believe everything happens for a reason, it gets easier to accept your abilities.

Exercise 7-1: Transitioning

> - You want to make a smooth transition from your current state to your desired state. Encourage yourself by asking the following questions:
> - Are you free to express your unique gifts and talents in your present situation?
> - Does your present situation reflect your purpose?
> - What have you been told all of your life that holds you back?
> - What are you tired of hearing from others?
> - What have you done or pursued in your life that was the result of what someone else wanted from you?
> - What is the one thing that needs to change to get the energy moving in the direction of your desired state?
> - What state of being makes you feel energized, inspired, and motivated?
> - Envision your ultimate life with no restrictions—what does it look like? How does it feel?

To transition from your current situation to your ideal state, make one small change toward your ultimate goal. Once you experience success with that one thing, take another small step. Challenge the naysayers and the old recordings of doubt. The bottom line is that until you decide what you want, you cannot move forward toward manifestation. This is the most important aspect of changing your life. You really have to want it with your heart and soul. Knowing without a doubt that you want something is the only way to get it.

Understand what is motivating you to choose one path or another. Wanting more money alone will not give you what you want. Instead, focus on creating your life in a way that provides whatever you need whenever you need it. When you find your path, it feels right. When you do it, you are energized. When others criticize you for your choices, it does not matter, because it will feel right to you.

What is your definition of success? Is it yours or someone else's? For some it may include marriage and children. For others it may be the freedom to travel and explore the world. For still others, it is the accumulation of money. I have witnessed many hardworking, wealthy people who have never achieved true happiness. Money alone is not a sufficient condition for happiness. While it is a necessity, and great to have, by itself it cannot define what your life is to be. You must define your own success and what ultimately makes you happy. Those who speak of regret generally focus on the things they wish they had done; opportunities they should have taken, or times they had wasted based on what others wanted from them.

While you may get push-back and resistance from family and friends, once you confidently determine for yourself what success looks like for you and embrace it, they will begin to accept your decision. After all, those who truly love you simply want what is best for you and want you to be happy. Following your own path will lead you to happiness. If there is still an issue with your choice, then it is their issue to contend with, as long as you are independent of their financial support.

To get the most out of life, you need to define your true hopes and desires. Decide what kind of person you want to be and then manifest a life that coincides with those characteristics. This design of your future life-to- be may very well change over time as you learn and grow. Flexibility allows you to change the path you are on at any point in time. When you happen upon a new trail, one that begs to be explored, take a small detour for exploration purposes; it may open up a new path that you had not considered. With that one decision, excitement replaces doubt, and you walk faster down the trail to see where it might lead. Try going part of the way in at first to test how you feel about the terrain. If it feels good, go deeper; if it is not the right trail or you want to try yet another before deciding which one you like best, adjust your course accordingly. Make the most of opportunities that arise and take the journey that feels right for you.

Your Mission, Vision, & Values

It is easier to manifest when what you want is in alignment with your soul's mission. A clear definition of your mission, vision, and values goes a long way in putting you on the path to achieving what you want in your life. Companies do this to define their goals and get everyone thinking in the same direction. It serves to direct the energy in a purposeful way toward manifesting the desired goal. When applied to you as a person, it serves as a moral compass to keep you moving on the course you have set for yourself. It may be something you express in your work, yet this goes beyond the way you earn your livelihood; this is stating what you stand for, what you want to contribute to the world, and how you want to express your purpose. It is a conceptualization of what your life represents.

Exercise 7-2: Develop Your Mission, Vision, and Value Statements

Grab your journal and your favorite writing instrument and sit quietly in a place that relaxes you where you can unplug from the world for a few hours and let's jump right in!

Mission (what you want to achieve/the goal): A mission states the purpose of your goal (the what and why). To formulate your mission, look beyond the obvious things such as salary and material possessions. It can be as long or as short as you would like. Start by writing everything that occurs to you and then whittle it down to capture the essence of the mission. An example is "To inspire and teach others to embrace their true nature."

Vision (how you want to be or how you want the world to be as a result of your efforts): Your vision points to your destination (where you want to go). It is a long-term vision of the future. Having a clear vision will motivate you and move your energy forward. An example is, "A world where people are free to be themselves."

Values (who you are and how you want to behave): Your core values describe the beliefs that guide every action you take. They are the beliefs that you hold sacred. It is the way you want to live your life. Some examples could be: Treat all people with respect. Act with honesty, integrity, and in the best interest of yourself and others.

Once written, keep your mission, vision, and values statements in a place where you can often refer to them.

Still not sure? The hardest thing to do is figure out what you want! These questions may help.

- What did you want to be when you were 7 years old? Kids know who they are, and then they get derailed.

- What is your ideal environment to live and work in? For example, a quiet environment with trees around me.

- What are your greatest strengths? Be honest. Now is not the time to be modest. Ask those you trust if you have difficulty seeing them for yourself.

- What activities give you energy? What are you truly passionate about? Community service, individual support of others, a cause or issue, a particular craft or sport?

Once you are clear about what you want, create a plan. Defining what you want must be followed by action. There can be no success without action. Outline the steps you want to take toward your desires, and give yourself a timeframe in which to complete each phase. In this way, you are setting the energy of being in the process of manifesting, rather than waiting for something to happen. Make progress each day, even if it is a small, simple action like a follow-up phone call or some research. It will get you closer to your ultimate desire.

Track your progress so that you can see how applying your energy is moving you forward. Feel the energy build with the momentum you create with each step.

Follow these guidelines to get your energy moving toward your ideal life:

- **Know What You Want:** Get clear. Translate the mental list of what you want to do into a written list of potentials and possibilities.

- **Do It:** Try each idea on your list one at a time, to get some experience and see how you feel about them. If you cannot have direct, physical experience with it, envision it clearly and try walking through it in your mind to see how it feels. You have to try the things that you think you want to do to avoid ending up with a lot of "what ifs." There is nothing more liberating than actually doing things you are passionate about. By doing things you love (or think you love) you make your dream come true, or you stop wasting time on things you thought you wanted, because you can learn that it is not what you really want. Eliminate the options that do not feel right to you.

- **Surround Yourself with Positive People:** This is one of the greatest things you can do for yourself. If you surround yourself with positive people or like-minded people, they help to propel you forward. Another good way to increase your energy and skill is to surround yourself with people who are adept at something you would like to do or who already live an inspired life. Their energy will lift yours and you can learn much in the process. You energetically attract these people by shifting your energy into higher vibrational levels.

- **Leverage:** Know what you are good at and use it to its maximum potential. Know what your weak points are and get help in that area by learning more about it or by delegating that particular task to someone else. Learn how to fully utilize all available resources around you. Understand your limitations or challenges and work around them. Find alternatives if needed.

- **Lose the fear:** Use the delays, challenges, and difficulties as lessons to be learned. They usually shed light on something that was previously hidden and needed to be brought to the surface. Determine what lesson is inherent in the situation and modify your efforts accordingly.

- **Check in with yourself:** How does it feel when you visualize your ideal life? Can you breathe easier? Do you feel lighter? Do you smile? If something does not feel right, shift your perspective and look at it objectively until you can get to feeling comfortable with the energy.

Accept the fact that you have the power to create the life you want, take responsibility, and take action!

Chapter 8 – Psychic Awareness and Energy: Tap into Your Inner Guidance

Inner Guidance

Inner guidance can help you take back your power by listening to and trusting yourself, giving you the freedom to cultivate your unique self, and so creating your destiny. I promise you that there absolutely are wonderful aspects of yourself trying to get out! You have knowledge, intuitive ability (yes, you do), and aspirations waiting to be transformed into wisdom, inner guidance, and a meaningful, fulfilling life.

How do you know that you have intuitive ability? Consider how many times you received a *knowing*; something that you felt in your gut to be true, but ignored it, and then everything went wrong. Or a time when you followed the little voice in the back of your mind and everything went right. That is your intuition. Everyone has this ability; it is just a matter of degree. We all truly have six senses, it is just that the sixth, that of intuition, has been swept aside as being the realm of professional psychics. Every single person has this ability. It was our ancestors' way of getting information they needed to survive. Today, this ability is more important than ever to navigate the complexities inherent in life. Intuition guides us without giving us any explanation as to why we are to trust it. That is what makes it so difficult to take action on the information we receive in this way. We want to know why and how the information fits into a logical schema.

What is the biggest benefit of developing your intuitive ability? Things will go more smoothly, you will increase your level of self-trust, and thereby your confidence level.

Let us take a look at how your intuitive abilities are most likely to present themselves.

We Are All Intuitive

The way your intuitive ability manifests is intimately tied to your true nature. It is tied to your knowledge set and to your strongest mundane ability. Emotionally sensitive people *feel* the information. Those who are more cerebral will most likely get messages by way of *thoughts*. If you have a gift for knowing what is physically wrong with someone, then the message will come through as a physical sensation or even *seeing* the anomaly on the body. It is valuable to explore where your strongest abilities are and what circumstances enhance them.

Exercise 8-1: Notice Patterns

Answer the following questions based on your past and current experiences.

Are you more sensitive at certain times of year?

In certain situations? (When you feel threatened, for example)

When you are in a certain mood? (Peaceful, happy, depressed, etc.)

With certain people or types of people?

Is there a particular type of information you tend to get (relationship, finance, career)?

Intuition happens on a daily basis, yet often the messages are ignored, minimized, or not trusted. You get guidance throughout the day, those flashes of insight that tell you who is calling when the phone rings (without looking at caller ID), what your children are doing or experiencing, a "knowing" about the best way to handle a situation. It happens so naturally and subtly that you may not notice it, or you may acknowledge the message and then choose to ignore it or distrust that it is correct.

Barriers to listening to the messages include fear of what might come through, such as visions of an accident, doubting that the message has any validity, and allowing personal feelings or thoughts to get in the way of the message. People telling you that you are crazy or saying that intuitive ability is evil also serve to shut down your natural gift. All of these obstacles serve to reduce the ability to objectively receive the message and to act on it. There are times when the message is misunderstood or missed altogether as a result of the noise generated by internal thoughts and the external bombardment of information and energies. Seek to overcome distractions by tapping into the important intuitive information that is all around you while separating it from the noise. This takes practice and a deep self-knowing, so you can *feel* when it is an actual message versus when it is merely a thought generated from anxiety or hope.

Tapping in

Intuitive information may be derived from

- Universal Energy (Spirit, God, Source, etc.), where there is a grand storehouse of information, a virtual repository of imprints from all thoughts, events, and circumstances that ever existed. You can pull information from this energy any time you need a new perspective.

- The person you are seeking to get information about. The person must be open to allowing you to "see" any messages that can be gleaned from their aura (energy field). Some people shield against this type of disclosure, even when asking for a reading. Do not be surprised if there are certain people who you cannot get information from.

- Your Higher Self. These messages may come across as sensing when something does not *feel* right, or when you get an idea from out of the blue that helps you move past an obstacle.

- Objects and places that hold energy previously imprinted up on them.

How Messages Come Through

When a message comes through, it can take a variety of forms. Your intuitive gift may present itself as an image. You might see a scenario play out in your mind's eye or get an image associated with whatever you are asking about. Images of people, places, or things may appear to you. Along with the image, there may be an emotional component as well. For example, you may see an argument between two people and feel their frustration or anger with each other. At the same time, your gift may be primarily emotional, wherein you sense depression, joy, anxiety, or other emotions emanating from the person or situation you seek to get a message about. It is important to be able to differentiate between your own feelings and the intuitive sensing of another's.

For some people, messages come through as physical sensations. I pick up a lot of information physically, that is, if my client is having shoulder pain, I will get an ache in my shoulder or feel a heaviness in my chest which turns out to be the client's reaction to stress. During one reading in particular, I became short of breath, and when my client saw it, she said that she was prone to panic attacks. Grounding is important to minimize or avoid this type of experience. By using grounding and protection methods, you are able to receive the information about a physical issue without having to experience the full blown extent of the malady. Whenever you are connected to someone's energy field, there is an energy exchange and you must protect yourself. An instant grounding technique is to uncross your legs and feel your feet on the floor. For advanced grounding techniques, refer to pp. 24 - 28.

Another type of intuitive sensation is a physical reaction, such as chills or gooseflesh on the arms or neck that serves as a personal trigger indicating something is right or wrong. It can also reflect what is being picked up from someone, as with a particular type of intuitive insight or associated with certain energies.

A former police officer shared with me that his gift and his ability to interpret his intuitive sensations developed over time. As a rookie, he would get certain feelings but not understand what they were telling him. Years later, he would have a sense of what a person was about even if he was unaware they had committed a crime. He learned to listen to what he was feeling because nine out of ten times his feeling was correct. This is a great example of how your area of expertise can enhance the type of intuitive messages that come through.

When something was wrong, the indicator was a chill that started at the back of his neck (not fear) and worked its way down his back. He felt the chill as he pulled over a car with two men in it. Nothing on the surface was apparently wrong. He went back to his vehicle and ran their information. It turned out they did an armed robbery the day before and killed someone. In another case, he saw a man, and even though there was nothing outstanding about him, he had a bad feeling that something was not right. It turned out that he had just robbed a house. As a result, the perpetrator was caught within 5 minutes of committing the crime.

An opposite sensation would occur when the person could be trusted even without previous knowledge of the individual. He would get a warm feeling in the center of his back. One explanation is that the feeling is originating at the solar plexus chakra. This is a center of energetic protection, so the warming reflected that he would not need to protect himself.

Intuitive messages can also present themselves through the other five senses. The same police officer had intuitive experiences with taste and smell that occurred only when searching buildings for a suspect. He could "smell" the energy, as opposed to a physical body odor. In one case, he *smelled* that there was somebody in the room being searched, but did not see anyone there. He did not know where the suspect was, but allowed himself to be guided by the intensity of the *smell*, and then got a bitter taste in his mouth. That is when he found the suspect hiding in the drop ceiling of a huge department store. He noticed that searching for someone prompted a different intuitive reaction than other situations. Listening to his intuitive guidance enhanced his ability to perform his job and likely saved his life many times.

There are times when people or things may look brighter or darker. The association made to each of these is very personal, so track how the energy is being perceived to get a deeper understanding of its meaning for you.

Your gift may present itself as thoughts that come seemingly from nowhere. If this is your tendency, it is very important to know yourself well to be able to distinguish a thought that is coming from your brain or what you already know, versus a thought that comes from another source. For me, thoughts that are messages come in a way that is not connected to anything I may be currently thinking. It feels different, more like a deep knowing.

Trusting the Message

Once you are able to recognize how you tend to get messages, the key is to trust what is coming through. The ability to differentiate what you "know" from what you are "getting" helps you determine the accuracy and validity of the message. Take note of what a regular thought feels like versus what that "little voice" tells you. How many times did a bit of information come to you, seemingly out of nowhere, and you say it only to have someone reply, "How do you know that?" You inevitably reply with something like, "I just know." And you do. This is not a function of the logical mind, but rather a higher knowing from the Universe or from your Higher Self.

Once you confirm that it is a valid message and not an emotional or logical reaction to a situation, then follow the guidance...even if it does not make sense. Think of times when this has happened to you. You are going through a normal day, and then something *tells you* to do something other than what you are planning to do. You decide to let logic prevail, only to find out that if you had listened to that *little voice* things would have gone a lot smoother.

There was a time when I was packing to facilitate sessions at a women's retreat in the mountains. As I packed, the *little voice* said, "Baby wipes." I heard it, but ignored it. I do not buy baby wipes, and so it seemed odd. Also, I did not have time to stop at the store and finish other things I needed to do before leaving for three days. We got up to the location, and there had been torrential rains all week. Many roads were flooded. The building's water supply came from a well, which had caved in from all the rain; we had no running water all weekend. We ended up bathing with bottled water, and baby wipes would have been good to have! So be careful not to dismiss a message simply because it seems silly or because it does not fit in with your plans.

Techniques to Get Messages At Will

When I was young, I used to see colors around random people and experience psychic peaks in the autumn months. During that time, I was profoundly aware and open to getting all kinds of messages from the people around me, as well as receiving higher guidance on a regular basis. Once the autumn turned to winter, the peak receded and I was left to try to pull information, to no avail. It became a quest to develop my intuition to the point where it could be used consistently and with a high degree of accuracy. Here are some ways that you can even out your ability and use it whenever you want to.

Tools—A Very Personal Choice

When I began using the Tarot at a very young age, it helped to even out my psychic peaks. The cards allowed me to understand how I was moving my energy in order to pick up information. I also discovered that it was important for me to have the right deck, one that was aligned with my vibrational pattern so that I could easily use it to get information. I found that certain decks blocked my energy and were not effective tools for me. When I added Reiki training to that, my awareness was heightened, and my ability increased once again. I share many experiences and explain my free-form method of card reading in my book *The True Nature of Tarot: Your path to personal empowerment.*

Finding the tool that works for you is a very personal choice. I use many tools in addition to Tarot that include other types of card decks and oracles, pendulums, muscle testing, astrology, runes, and books (bibliomancy). I have even designed two tools—Insight Stones® and Pathways: An interactive journey of self-discovery* (both can be seen at http://www.DianeWing.com/new/Pathways.php and http://www.DianeWing.com/new/InsightStones.php)—to organize my esoteric knowledge and use it in a way that enhances the messages I seek. It is worthwhile to take time to try a variety of tools to see how and if they work for you. You will know it is the right one when the information seems to flow as a result of using it.

Do not limit yourself to tools that can be purchased. I know many readers who use tools that are outside of the mainstream such as shells, bones, tea leaves, and even trees. Others I know are psychometrists who get information by holding an object belonging to the person who wants the reading and pulling information from it. One day a friend of mine decided to pick up a leaf from the ground and see what she could get from it. She had never been called to a leaf to do this work before. It was the right energy, for she received very accurate messages regarding the question she posed. Explore any option that seems to call you to it and try it out. Do not let an "odd" tool stop you from using it. Being drawn to it is a form of intuitive guidance. Trust it.

Divination as a Personal Expression of Universal Energy

The idea of divination has been equated with predicting the future. The occult meaning of divination is "to connect to the divine." We are capable of receiving messages from Spirit so that we may act in accordance with Divine Will. As long as we have personal will which manifests as free will, then we are capable of creating our future rather than having it predicted for us. Your path can change simply by making one decision over another. Readings can indicate energies that are likely to manifest given the current state of affairs, yet we have the ultimate power to change that, regardless of what Divine Will dictates.

The practice of divination is a highly personal act, reflecting your unique connection to Spirit. The tools you select, the interpretations you apply, and the types of information that comes through are all indicative of where you are in your journey and the way you interact with Spirit. It is a way to release your Inner Magick. As you move forward on your path, your tools may change, your understanding will increase, and the depth of the messages you receive will deepen in accordance with your personal development and knowledge.

Over many years of working with and developing the skills of practitioners, I have encountered an amazing array of approaches to divination. All of us bring unique perspective to the practice. Some feel emotions from other people (empathic), some get messages about people by holding objects (psychometry), others are telepathic and can hear people's thoughts, and still others are connected to nature through the ground, the trees, or wild animals. I have met a couple of practitioners who use bones to pull the information—one uses small bones of chickens, the other uses one large bone. There are many who read cards, whether tarot, specialized decks, or playing cards; this is called cartomancy. The use of planetary energies is the main tool of astrologers. Others use a pendulum or divining rod. Runes are a fairly common practice using ancient glyphs to lead the practitioner to the information. Some practitioners read auras or energy fields and can see colors that indicate health and emotional factors about a person. Still others connect with the energies of those who have transitioned from the physical plane.

Volumes have been written on all sorts of divination methods. The truth is that nearly anything can be used as a tool to open to messages. All tools are valid, for they are simply that: tools to open the connection between you and the wisdom of Spirit. They have no power in and of themselves. The tendency toward one form or another may be cultural, hereditary, or simply a natural inclination. Finding the tool that most resonates for you can happen by chance or you may go on a search for the best way to connect to the Divine.

It may be that you do not require a tool in order to move the energy in a way that brings messages to you accurately and consistently. Some simply close their eyes and ask. For others the messages come through loud and clear during certain times of the year or in certain circumstances. A tool can enhance the ability to pull information at will.

The types of information that come through are as varied as the tools themselves. Some can sense weather disruptions and other natural events. It is valuable to explore where your strongest abilities are and what circumstances enhance them. Some are adept at relationship readings, vocational readings, or health readings. Others connect with the energies of those who have passed on to address grief issues for their clients. As you practice, take note of what is most likely to come through.

Many times it is connected to your personal body of knowledge, something that you have studied in the mundane realm. A doctor may intuitively diagnose a patient, despite the absence of expected symptoms or a hospice worker may be adept at dealing with spirits attempting to cross over. With my background in psychology, I tend to pick up on the aspects of a person that create blocks to progress. As in my previous example, a policeman may sense the criminal nature of a person. A realtor may have the gift of energetically matching buyers with the right home. The more you know about, the more types of information you can intuitively discern.

Some circumstances can block your ability to pull information. Fear of seeing something upsetting may block messages. You can ask Spirit to show you certain types of information or ask that you do not see disturbing visions. Before beginning a reading, ask that the information come through for the highest good of the inquirer. Other blocks happen when novices are so focused on using the tools correctly and applying the "right" meaning that they are unable to flow and derive messages beyond any traditional meaning.

Traditional interpretations are wonderful as a resource for foundational understanding. At the same time, I strongly encourage you to trust your own guidance as to what message is trying to come through, regardless of whether or not it matches with the "official" version. Reading about the interpretations of one author over another should never supersede what you feel in your deepest intuitive guidance. Trusting what you are getting is a matter of practice and validating the accuracy in order to increase your self-confidence.

To enhance the flow of information, see if there are any environmental aspects that work best for you. Natural environments versus man-made, noisy versus quiet, bright light versus dim; notice how you feel when you are in varying circumstances and take note of whether you are more open to the flow of information or if you are more likely to close yourself off. Also, your clothing may have some influence on your ability to pull information, such as wearing natural or synthetic fabrics, light or dark clothing, fully covered or skin revealed. Test yourself in a variety of circumstances and see which improves your ability to receive information.

Another measure for enhancing the flow of information is to see how the message comes through. Do you tend to "feel" the information or to "see" it? When feeling the information, does it show up as a physical sensation as in pain where the person you are reading feels it? Or do you tend to sense the texture of the energy, as agitated, constricted, or beaming? When seeing the information, does it show up in the tool you are using as with cards or in the pattern of the shells, or do you see it in your mind's eye like a movie playing? When this occurs, are you likely to speak faster as you provide the message download or does your body relax and you speak more slowly? Using these indicators can let you know when you are getting a true message from Spirit or if it coming from your own framework.

Knowing yourself is the key to accurate and successful means of divination, whether getting messages for yourself or for someone else. When performing this service for another person (as a practitioner), it is critical to get out of the way of the message and not put your context on it. It does not matter if you can make sense of the information; your role is to objectively transmit the message to the inquirer. Without self-awareness, the messages are imparted subjectively, carrying with them the beliefs and ideologies of the practitioner. To minimize incorporating your "stuff" into a reading, clear yourself energetically and emotionally before performing a reading (or any other type of service for that matter). At the same time, your life philosophy and belief system will come through in the way you impart the message. An optimistic practitioner will provide hope, while a cynical person will convey information with a sense of doom.

Major responsibility comes with the practice of divination. People who need information are willing to hand over their power to you during the session. Make sure that you help them understand that the next move is up to them and that you are merely asking Spirit for the information on their behalf. Those who are drawn to you will be attracted to your particular style and the kind of information you tend to call forth.

As you increase your self-awareness and your self-development, your abilities as a practitioner and your unique expression of the divine will grow stronger. Finding your personal divination style is a powerful way of discovering your true self.

Asking

"Ask and you shall receive" is absolutely true. If you do not ask the question, you will not get any answers. Also, if you do not ask the right question, you will not get the information you need. The best way to go about this is to request an answer from the Universe in the form of guidance, showing you the way, or giving you a download of how to accomplish something you have been struggling with. Keep it simple and to the point. You can pray on it, meditate on it, or simply ask as you are going through your daily routine.

Pose the question as an open-ended statement such as, give me a message about... or guide me to... This way, the answer will likely be comprehensive as opposed to asking if something is right or wrong, good or bad. Always ask "for your highest good." Of course, in times requiring a quick answer, beginning your question with "should I" or "is it in my best interest to" will put you on the right track. You will experience an immediate feeling of acceptance or discomfort; follow that feeling.

The more you practice asking, the faster the answers will come. They can come in the form of a gentle thought that floats into your mind or a flash of insight. One of my students gets messages through song lyrics, numerological indicators (such as certain numbers on a license plate), or through visual indicators such as photos sent to her electronically or even billboards or signs on buses. Stay aware of how your messages come to you.

Exercise 8-2: Practice

Practice is essential to get the flow of information coming to you on a regular basis. Try this exercise and see how you do:

Pair up with someone you do not know; if this is not possible, find a friend or relative who will act as the inquirer and try to separate what you know about that person from what comes through during the exercise.

Face each other.

"Ask" for a message that is important for the person to know right now, for their highest good.

Do not "edit" the message or try to make sense of it, just say what comes through, even if it does not make sense to you.

The important thing here is to stay objective. The message is not for you, it is for the other person, and so to simply say it as it is *told* to you will give the person the right message, and they will understand it. During one of my classes, a student doing the reading got an image of a horse farm and the person living at that horse farm. The student who got the message was hesitant to say it, because it did not make sense to her and thought it was not an important message, but the inquirer did have a horse and felt that living on a horse farm would be a dream come true. Do not judge the message; simply allow it to come and say it. You will be surprised.

Track Results: The best way to find trends and patterns in your inner guidance is to track your results. Use a journal or a spreadsheet to keep track of the following:

Note the day and time when you get a "message"

Include your "state of mind"

Write down the outcome—validate "message"

How did the message come through (visual, emotional, thought, etc.)

And, as always, fight the urge to doubt. In developing your intuitive sense, the hardest part is trusting the accuracy of what comes through.

Your Universal Self is derived from the ability to tap into The Source and through it, to reveal your own true nature. Self-awareness is fundamental to receiving messages from the Source Energy. You can listen to many opinions, read many books, but it comes down to what makes sense for you as an individual. Only you can make choices that are best for you. Your energetic health depends on strengthening the connection with Source through your subconscious mind and bringing it fully into the conscious mind in order to act on it.

Once again, I want to emphasize that messages revealed through astrology, tarot, or any other system of divination are meant to show you the energies held within the situation, where you are now, and what needs to be addressed. These give you an alternate perspective, so you can see beyond your personal limitations. It can help to generate alternatives or to test your current options. It is not to predict your future; it is to show you the energies around you and the potential of your choices. These are tools by which to receive guidance from Spirit and your higher self. You can launch your training through many magickal systems. They are all structures and symbolic representations of ways to reach enlightenment and connect with Source. They seek to outline paths and challenges, as well as virtues to attain. But the system itself is not to be embraced as much as how it feels for you as a guideline toward integration with your higher self.

Chapter 9 – Other Energies

We are a combination of various energies, each present by degree. Some energies may dominate our nature and others will surface only on special occasions. We are the essence of the concept of polarity. Polarity differs from duality in that each pole has the essence of the other contained within it. There is a range and degree of each aspect housed within the other, inseparable.

Polarity

A continuum of polarities exists within us, and what we manifest is a combination of these polarities in varying degrees. Nothing exists in a pure state; everything blends to form unique and vibrant combinations. The physical and metaphysical aspects inherent in the energy that surrounds us is where the polarity begins; the power generated by opposites yet has the essence of each opposite held within it.

The duality inherent in nature serves to produce energetic interactions as seen in the interaction of positrons and electrons within the atomic structure, in magnetic fields that display positive and negative polarities, in the light of day and the dark of night, the sun and the moon, and in the human forms of male and female. In each case, both aspects are necessary to create balance and promote harmony in the world. Energy continuously seeks balance.

On the metaphysical side, it is the Yin (moon, female, cold, dark, submission) and Yang (sun, male, heat, light, projective) energies working to balance active with passive. It is the energies of the god and goddess and the forces of conscious and subconscious. Each of us contains all of these aspects, traits, and characteristics within ourselves. Each individual is the duality, the dichotomy, reflecting the potential of the Ultimate Energy Source. We are able to tap into the Source to bring these aspects together for our highest good or most devastating demise.

Nothing is separate; nothing can in and of itself stand alone and effectively produce the desired result. Everything is connected.

Some examples are:

Analytical/Creative:

Within each creative act is a measure of data analysis taking place, pulling together information about a particular perspective and organizing it in a way that expresses the essence of that information. The system of Tarot is a creative expression of the metaphysical laws that apply to the human condition and its relationship to the Divine. The act of interpreting the artistic renderings of symbols and concepts as they appear on the cards is analytical. At the more analytical end of this polarity, a scientist who is gathering data and designing a system to make sense of the information uses the creative faculty in order to create a visual or conceptual means of expressing the results.

Physical/Mental

: An athlete is predominantly physical in the act of performing his expertise, yet a strong mental component is essential to perform at the top of his game. Negative self-talk can diminish an athlete's chances of winning. For those who are performing primarily in a mental/academic capacity, research has shown that daily exercise is important to optimum brain function.

Left Brain/Right Brain

Some individuals are right-brain (creative) dominant, some are left-brain (logical) dominant, and some use both hemispheres of the brain equally. When one or the other is dominant, the subordinate hemisphere is still active and contributing to the task at hand, albeit in a less prominent way.

Congruent Energy:

When the Universe decides that it is time to reveal into the world a new philosophy, invention, or concept, individuals from all over the planet come up with similar thoughts. Timelines throughout history show that certain important inventions occurred simultaneously in different countries that had no way of communicating with each other.

A long list of examples of this is available at
http://en.wikipedia.org/wiki/List_of_multiple_discoveries.

The seamless whole theory helps to explain the mechanism by which this can occur. This is the idea that reality is non-local (Herbert, 1985), and that everything is connected. Two seemingly unrelated molecules in space can affect each other's motions; they are interrelated and connected by an unseen force. The actions of one influence the actions of the other. Similarly, this occurs between beings on Earth. Humans are becoming more aware of how their thoughts, feelings, and actions can elevate or diminish the vibratory level of the whole planet.

The fear and hate that terror releases into the world brings down the vibration of our entire planet. To reduce this effect, each person can take inventory of his or her own emotions, thoughts, and actions. Cleanse yourself of lower vibrations and seek thoughts, feelings, and behaviors that produce higher, more positive vibrations. Maximizing the number of individuals who are willing to perform this exercise would increase the chance of successfully reducing the instance of war and adversity. By focusing on compassion, understanding, and cultivating inner peace, we can raise our own vibration, as well as the vibration of those around us.

Collaborative Energy

Everything is about integration and interconnectivity. Nothing has a separate aspect. All components are essential when seeking to understand anything, including the self. You cannot work successfully on one part of an issue without working on the other parts simultaneously. For example, when a person focuses on losing weight, diet and exercise address the physical component of the problem. In most cases, this is insufficient to achieve the desired goal and maintain it. To be successful, the emotional, mental, and spiritual aspects of food and self-image need similar attention while addressing the physical issues. One feeds the other, one affects the other, one interacts with the other to create unique interconnections in the way it affects your life and the problem at hand. It also influences what your external reality looks like.

The physical body is the realm of health and sustenance; the mental body houses thoughts and beliefs; the emotional body houses feelings; and the spiritual body provides connectivity to the Divine. All have different vibrational patterns and all work together to give the being a complete energetic profile. An imbalance from any one of these energetic bodies affects the vibratory patterns of the rest. An improvement in any one of these energetic bodies influences the well-being of the rest. When you feel better physically, your emotional body responds favorably; when your emotional body is free of discord, your mental clarity increases. With mental clarity, your connection to the Divine is stronger. Everything is connected and impacts one another.

When helping others, rewards may not come directly from the place you direct your energies. For example, you do something kind for a particular person. That person may not do something in return, but the reward comes to you from an unexpected source. When I was a teenager, I regularly helped my friends when they were having a difficult time. One day I was walking around New York City and the rawhide shoelace on my boots broke. I only had a dollar and some change in my pocket. I went into a shoe store to price rawhide shoelaces. It turned out that they cost more than I had with me. The sales person came over to me and asked if I needed help. I told him what I needed, but that I did not have enough money to make the purchase and went to leave the store. He stopped me and gave me a pack of the shoelaces I needed. I tried to give him the money, but he refused to take it. I was so grateful and thanked him profusely. The interaction confused me; I could not figure out why he would do that for me, a complete stranger, with absolutely no expectation of ever seeing me again. It was years later that I realized it was a function of the Law of Return: that what I put out into the Universe will come back to me—but not necessarily in a form I expect.

Everything connects to everything else—all actions, thoughts, and intentions—so this should come as no surprise. A direct line from one event to the other is unnecessary to glean the rewards that come from helping others. Being in high service to others, without expectation of reward beyond the seeing their joy, cultivates a generally high vibration that attracts abundance to you.

When two or more people simultaneously focus on the same thing, it increases the likelihood that it will manifest. When a group of people meditate together regularly, the instance of crime is reduced in that particular geographic area. If an organization understands the goal they are trying to reach and works collaboratively to achieve it, they will succeed and more quickly than if their energies are scattered. When a couple has the same life goals in mind, they work together to create the life they want together. When a client and I have a flow of energy between us, the session is energizing and productive. When objects with like energies are combined, they enhance the overall effect of that energy.

Think of times when you have collaborated to create an outcome versus when there was resistance. With collaboration you feel energized; with resistance, fatigued.

When Energies Collide

Energy cannot be accumulated and wasted at the same time. Putting energy toward situations and sources that do not align with your goals is wasted. As your energy shifts, some friends will separate from your energy and others more closely aligned with the raised vibrational level will enter. Draining relationships are painlessly removed and inspiring connections come gently in. Without judgment, without arguments or resentment, and without addressing the situation, these relationships naturally dissolve. To create these smooth transitions, all semblance of resistance must be removed; that is, any unwillingness to let go of the relationship and any fear of being alone. New energy can come in when the old has been dispatched.

Some energies conflict when there are too many conditions and variables. When there are too many people involved or too many conflicting goals, there will be difficulty in having an effect. In this case, focus on the changes that need to be made within you and allow the other energies involved to run their course.

When energies feel like they are at odds with each other, suspend your efforts, take a step back, and let go of any preconceived notions or outcomes. Then allow the Universe to work it out.

Chapter 10 – Twenty Tips for Successful Living

There is a lot of information out there about success; success in business, success in relationships, success at work. Most strategies focus on specific outcomes and then we wonder why there is no balance in life. Success may only manifest in one aspect of life. The following tips are applicable to all facets.

Over time, choose to focus on one, several, or all of the tips. Read through each section and see which ones resonate most strongly for you at this time. Revisit this report periodically to gauge where you are versus where you could be.

1. Everyone and everything is your teacher. With each encounter, there is an opportunity to learn and grow. From family and friends to those you work with or even those you meet by chance in a store or on the street, these people have come into your life to demonstrate lessons that are needed at that particular time. Use the relationships in your life to uncover deep life lessons.

Action Step: Whether the interaction is positive or negative, ask yourself what purpose is being served by the encounter. Is it to remind you of simple pleasures or childhood joys? It is to bring your attention to an aspect of yourself that requires further examination? Do the dynamics in your family reveal an underlying issue that needs to be addressed?

2. Knowing yourself is the most important purpose. Striving for self-knowledge and self-awareness is a lifelong quest. Around every bend there is another opportunity to more deeply understand the Self. Many tools, assessments, and approaches, both traditional and nontraditional, are available to enhance knowledge of the Self. There are many benefits that make self-knowledge a worthwhile pursuit, including having more control over your life by knowing what you want and do not want. You are more likely to make appropriate choices and generate viable alternatives when you have a solid understanding about who you are. This knowledge promotes inner peace, as self-doubt is replaced by self-awareness. Tapping into your core self enables you to act with purpose, withstand stress, and be resilient during difficult times.

Action Step: Use the exercises in this book to kick-start your journey. Use self-exploration tools. Then journal, read, and observe yourself in a variety of situations to understand the patterns in your life. Ask trusted friends for feedback or consult a professional to go deeper into your self-discovery.

3. Gratitude for all that is in your life is a necessary condition for happiness.
 When everything is going well, it is easy to be grateful for what has been given you. In times of difficulty and distress, gratitude is a bit more challenging to muster, yet these are the times when it is most important to display gratitude. Realize that challenges are put into your life to serve as lessons and to reveal your strengths and weaknesses. Be grateful for these times, for growth will not occur without them. It is possible to turn distress into happiness by using the situation as a catalyst for inspiration to improve your circumstances, approach, or outlook. When you know that you are capable of moving beyond problems, you are strengthened and ready to meet the next challenge that comes along. Feeling strong and capable in the face of adversity promotes a happy perspective in both good times and bad.

Action Step: Make a list of what is in your life that you are grateful for, no matter how small or trivial it may seem at first. The more you write, the more you will realize how fortunate you are. Example: Your health, a roof over your head, the mental capacity to learn, soft sheets, the love of others, etc.

4. The world reflects back that which you project onto it. If you feel like the world is out to get you and that nothing could possibly go right, then that is exactly what the world will show you. There will be continuous evidence presented to you to support your position. When the world looks dark and people do not treat you with respect, it is likely that your view of yourself is similar. With a change of perspective, it is possible to change the way the world reacts to you. It is not about changing the world, but rather changing the way you perceive it and yourself. When you begin to see potential in yourself and the beauty in the world, this is what is reflected back to you. In the words of Gandhi, "Be the change you wish to see in the world."

Action Step: Take a hard look at yourself. Are you behaving and presenting yourself in a way that supports how you'd like to be viewed by others? Are you judging others in a way that you do not want to be judged? Then look at the outer world and seek out bright spots in the darkness, such as focusing on people laughing and having fun, finding beauty in nature at the local park, or taking an interest in others.

5. Tap into your intuitive side and follow your inner guidance. Everyone has intuition. Some use it more effectively than others. The key to using this gift successfully is self-trust. Your inner guidance is the most valuable asset you possess. The development of this personal tool allows you to be self-sufficient and make choices that are in your best interest and for your highest good. You have probably experienced this phenomenon; suddenly you "know" something or get a "feeling" that you should take a particular course of action. For example, you will be on your way out and suddenly a thought will come across your mind that tells you to grab a certain magazine with a particular ad in it. Generally you will ignore the advice and leave the house without it. When you get to your destination, there is someone there who could have used the information from the magazine. Things go more smoothly when you listen to your inner voice.

Action Step: Track when an intuitive message comes through and write down the result. In this way, you will begin to differentiate between a simple thought and an actual intuitive message.

6. Take responsibility for your decisions and their consequences. Accept responsibility! It is your responsibility to make informed choices, to decide which options are appropriate and take action, and to accept responsibility for the consequences of your actions and decisions. It is up to you to choose harmony over chaos. Certain decisions you make will lead to worry and difficulty, while others will minimize adversity and produce happiness and rewards. Rely on your past experience with the decisions you have made. Ask for help when you need more information to make an appropriate choice and take the responsibility for your final decision. Use your intuitive guidance to confirm right action. Blaming others does not help you to grow and to make better choices next time around. Blaming others is an irresponsible way to go through life, when everything that happens to you is ultimately a result of your free will and the decisions you make. To be successful, it is important to self-assess and determine what went wrong and how to avoid the same mistake in the future.

Action Step: Consider how your choices have impacted outcomes in your life. Which decisions created an undesirable result? Which ones have proved to be the right choice? How did you arrive at the decision? Recall the process you used when the decision was beneficial and determine if it is appropriate to use going forward.

7. Everything happens for a reason. Nothing happens by chance. All occurrences are culminations of decisions, circumstances, and actions that came before them, either initiated by you or by someone or something outside of your sphere of influence. Everyone and everything is connected energetically and so what an individual does effects those around him, whether directly or indirectly. Even if it seems to have happened out of the blue, the situation was put into place as a result of many interactions, many out of your control, finally arriving in your life for you to determine the next action. It may come to you as a lesson to be learned or an important contact for you to make to achieve a goal.

Action Step: Be aware of what advantages are inherent in each encounter and circumstance. Take appropriate action to move your goals forward, to cultivate or extinguish certain relationships, or to learn from the experience.

8. Do not blindly accept what you are told (check in with yourself). There are many people and entities (companies, religions, programs) that claim to be experts in their particular area. While books may have been written and testimonials proclaimed, it is important for you to reach down and see how the information feels to you. Does it resonate with your experience? Is it something you would like to know more about, or do you reject the notion wholeheartedly? Do not follow blindly a concept that does not feel right to you.

Action Step: Consider the source, consider how the information applies to you and your goals, and consider how certain beliefs may benefit or limit you.

9. Pay attention. Every experience, interaction, thought, and feeling you have has the potential to enlighten, frighten, surprise, or delight. Do not miss out by ignoring what is going on around you and within you. Additionally, do not become so distracted by your cell phone, constant bombardments of information, and the list of things to do running through your mind that you zone out and make a poor decision, have an accident while driving, or alienate someone important to you.

Action Step: Practice staying in the moment. Turn off the electronics, including the radio and television, and observe what is going on around you. Try to notice things that you may have missed in the past due to distractions. Feel how focused you can be as you attend to the task at hand.

10. Consider how what you do affects others, for two major reasons: first, we are all connected, so if one person does something to cause discontent for another, it brings down the vibration of the entire energy field. Even something as simple as not paying attention when you are first at a traffic signal can delay all of the people behind you. Be considerate, use common courtesy, and think of how it affects you when others act selfishly or with total disregard of others. Second, whatever you put out comes back to you threefold , so whether you create discord and hurtful situations or peace and joy for others, it will come back to you stronger than the original energy in every aspect of your life.

Action Step: Take notice of how your actions affect those around you on a regular basis.

11. Get rid of the doom and gloom. Every time you complain, say something negative about yourself or someone else, adopt a pessimistic attitude, or thrive on the drama of others or what's on the news and in the media, you surround yourself with negativity. This negative energy will cloud and stain every aspect of your life, and you will end up asking yourself why the dark cloud is following you…you have invited it to join you on your journey! Create light and love in your life through gratitude and a positive outlook. Once your perspective changes, so will your circumstances and the way people react to you. Notice how the people who are attracted to you are those with a more optimistic outlook and success in their lives.

Action Step: Do not watch the news or participate in conversations with complainers for one week. See how you feel at the end of that period (more relaxed, less anxious, more hopeful).

12. Focus on the solution not the problem. Thinking about the problem grows it out of proportion and makes it feel insurmountable. Focusing on the solution sheds light on the problem and opens to the possibility of overcoming the obstacle. You will find that you become more hopeful and have a brighter outlook and clearer perspective when you think about solutions. Look to understand why the problem is in your life—there is a lesson in all challenges we face. The way we deal with issues that arise gives us information about the type of person we are and what we need to work on.

Action Step: Generate at least three options to deal with whatever issue has arisen. If you problem is large, cut it into segments that are easier to deal with and generate alternatives for each piece of the issue.

13. Be open to all possibilities. There are times when a thought pops into your head, but is immediately pushed away with the phrase, "I cannot do that because" or "That cannot happen because." Or when you ask someone for advice and they offer viable solutions only to be met by your negativity around the impossibility of accomplishing what was suggested. This is self-sabotage and creates a sense of being stuck. It also pushes people away, making them less likely to offer help in the future. The Universe provides ideas and visions to support us in achieving our desires and giving us what we need. Rather than thinking of all the reasons why something will not work, focus on how to make the ideas happen; if it feels right to you then invest yourself in its potential. Your belief, emotional passion, and visual imagery of the idea will help it to manifest.

Action Step: When you are experiencing a problem—you do not like where you live or work, for example—start generating alternatives to address it. Do not judge the options; simply write them down and think of ways that they could work. When a self-sabotaging thought pops up like "that will not work," push it aside and refocus on why it could work.

14. Smile. It is amazing the response you will get from others when you smile. People will want to be around you and their happiness quotient will rise along with yours. This brings joy to others as well as yourself. Your sense of wellbeing and that of the other person will be elevated as a result of this brief, positive interaction. It is especially powerful when you see someone who seems down in the dumps. Offering a smile can lift them enough to rekindle a sense of hope. The more of these small, joyous moments you can accumulate and propagate, the more likely you are to have happiness in your life and to bring happiness to others.

Action Step: Try it with strangers as you walk down the street; when your eyes meet, simply smile. In my experience, the person smiles back 98 percent of the time.

15. What you put out comes back to you threefold. While this tip is mentioned in tip number 10 above, it is worth mentioning again, as it is a critical concept for your success and happiness. By helping others, giving of yourself, and providing people with a positive experience, you improve your chances of receiving the support you need from the Universe and from others to achieve your desires. The energy you put out comes back similarly from places you do not expect. Let us say you do a good deed for Harry. The energetic reward will not necessary come back to you directly from Harry, but may come in the form of help and support from another source when you needed it most. If you are hurtful to someone, the negative backlash may not come back to you directly from that person, but could manifest in the form of another important relationship being compromised or the loss of something important to you. Choose to act in the highest good of yourself and others to raise the vibration of those around you and the planet in general, not just because of the karmic boomerang effect.

Action Step: Next time you help someone, notice how quickly the Universe reciprocates, what form it takes, and from whence the reward comes. Next time you do something that hurts another, notice how quickly the karmic backlash manifests, what form it takes, and how it relates to your negative action.

16. Be good to your body. We are spiritual beings, yet we are required to interact on the physical plane. Being respectful of the vessel that houses the spirit body is essential for success. Messages received from the Universe are processed cognitively, that is through the mind's eye, and if our body is not healthy, neither is our brain function. The likelihood of receiving important messages from the Universe and from the higher self diminishes with the deterioration of the mind and body. It also affects your energy level. Proper nutrition, sleep, and exercise are required to maintain a high energy level, which is critical for accomplishing all of the ideas and creative aspirations that are waiting to be acted upon.

Action Step: Evaluate for yourself, or with the help of a professional, your dietary, sleep, and exercise needs and modify your lifestyle accordingly. Many websites exist with tools to analyze what you are currently doing and providing guidance on ways to improve your health. RealAge.com has a tool to test your "real age" physically versus chronologically, and provides good health tips by medical experts.

17. Be a lifelong learner. As you change, your perceptions change, and the outer world looks different. With each bit of information learned, you expand your potential beyond what it was only moments ago, and increase your level of understanding in order to think beyond your former boundaries. Ignorance leads to mental limitations. Breaking beyond it is necessary in order to identify your purpose and direct your energy to achieve your goals. Knowing more expands awareness about yourself and others, as well as opens pathways to new ways of perceiving. Whether you are learning about external things that interest you or seeking a deeper understanding of yourself, you will ultimately benefit as your increased knowledge enriches your life path.

Action Step: To learn about your Self, try journaling to explore your reaction and experiences without judgment. Write down your perception of people and situations and look for patterns in the way you view the world. Consider how this perspective helps or hinders your ability to gain a deeper understanding of yourself. If you find it difficult to be objective through journaling, seek professional assistance to help you develop self-awareness. To learn about external topics, choose something you have always wanted to know more about. It could be anything—cooking, quilting, how pickles are made, philosophy, science—and take a class, watch a program, or read a book about your chosen subject. Do this frequently throughout your life.

18. Know what you are talking about! If you are claiming to be an expert or if you are going down a path where your knowledge is essential in guiding others (this relates to all occupations: contractor, caregiver, counselor, retail associate), know your business, know your product, know more than your customers or those you interact with. In this way, you will avoid embarrassment and will not sound like a fool. More importantly, people will trust you with their needs and want to do business with you.

Action Step: Choose one topic per week or month for which you'd like to expand your expertise. Search the Internet, talk to experts, and read up on the subject until you have a high comfort level. Share what you have learned with others to practice using the information, thereby assimilating what you have learned to increase retention.

19. Take control of your destiny! You have heard claims that this person or that method will reveal your life purpose and path. Do not believe it! The only one who can determine that is you. It is possible, and sometimes necessary, to seek assistance for guidance in discovering your life purpose, but claims of being able to tell you what that is should be taken with a grain of salt. There are also independent methods you can use to help reveal that, such as consulting with your higher self either alone or using a tool (Insight Stones or Pathways, for example), but only you can determine what your life's purpose is and which path is best for you to follow. Do not give up your power or allow others to determine your destiny. Develop self-awareness, and in that way, you will ultimately trust yourself to do what feels right for you and what you want out of life.

Action Step: There are several ways you can tap into this information: 1) Sit quietly, eyes closed, and ask yourself if the path you are currently on is the best one for you or if a different approach is needed; 2) Select a tool like Insight Stones to help you tap into your intuitive side to determine your path and purpose; and/or 3) Seek the assistance of a professional you feel comfortable with to explore possibilities and uncover the best path and identify your purpose.

20. Be yourself! Do not delude yourself by thinking that there is nothing special about you; that others have more to offer or are smarter or better looking, or that you have nothing to offer. Every person has unique gifts, talents, and mannerisms that beg to be discovered. Your special way of looking at the world, a particular ability you have, and the things that are important to you reflect who you are, what you can ultimately become, and what value you bring to the table. In order to see yourself more clearly, it is important to broaden the views of the Self and to elevate satisfaction levels with who you truly are. Everyone has something to contribute to the world. Each of us has the potential to achieve comfort within ourselves. As you observe your Self, you will unveil aspects of your true nature, allowing you to reach new levels of understanding, and increase self-satisfaction and enjoyment.

Action Step: Strive to appreciate your strengths and overcome weaknesses. Ask those you trust how they see you and about your challenges and opportunities. Take time to develop your special gifts and unique aspects of your personality. At times, it is valuable to have assistance in exploring the Self, developing your true nature, and learning methods of finding and using your special gifts. Contact me or visit my website at www.DianeWing.com to find out how we can work together to help you gain control of your destiny.

Conclusion

Energy is everywhere and in all things. You imprint your energies on everything you touch, imagine, and create. Your energy is imprinted on your car, your robe, your bedding, and your home. It is reflected in your business and in your work. It is tangible. People and animals can feel your vibrations and you can sense theirs.

I was watching a sitcom on television that had a scene where two women were in a bar trying to pick up men. All the men kept going over to one of the women and none were talking to the other one. She was puzzled by her lack of attraction, so she asked a man who walked right past her to the other woman why he had done so. He said that she was very attractive, but she had the "unavailable vibe," like she was already in a relationship. She was not in a committed relationship, although she had strong feelings for a particular man, hence the "vibe" she projected that blocked attracting others.

Stay aware of the kind of vibration you project; many times you think you are masking underlying motivations, yet others can feel them in the form of signals to approach, avoid, or proceed with caution. Remember this when you are left wondering why you must struggle to attract the right people into your life. Check-in with yourself or ask a trusted friend about the "vibe" you are giving off. It is possible to create an intentional stand-offish vibration or a welcoming one. Make sure you are consciously producing these energies in a way that serves your purpose.

Even the photographs you use for your personal and professional images carry energy with them that invite people to interact with you or repel them. Those who use professional pictures of themselves taken when they were very young as their headshot give off a vibration that they do not accept themselves in their current state. That photo carries old energies with it, projecting who you were rather than portraying who you are today, and the disconnect may create distrust among those you would like to do business with. Update your professional headshot every couple of years to reflect the shifts in your energy, the wisdom you have attained, and the presence you have cultivated.

During the time I was writing this book, I continued to unfold, experiencing many energetic shifts and realizations. Life is an amazing journey that allows the continuous morphing and shifting we are all capable of. Nothing stays the same. Nature dictates change and you are able to flow with those changes if you suspend resistance and follow the flow to shape your life. Since you began reading this book, your energy and vibrational level has shifted. Take the Wing Vibrational Quiz now and compare it with your initial vibrational level.

Music, objects, people, places, and nature all contain the energies of their true natures. Surround yourself with those energies and vibrations that align with what you envision for yourself. Knowing what they are is the first step, but an insufficient condition for using the energies in positive ways. Practice sensing and applying the energies; gain a deeper understanding of the world and see objectively so that you are able to move through your life without judgment, without fear, and without doubt. Your confidence will increase the more you validate what you perceive and as you follow your own guidance and that of Divine will.

As you go through life, your core self remains, yet your peripheral self changes. The energy that flows around you must be harnessed and dealt with, while the internal energy must be bolstered and transformed. Hard to change patterns of behavior are the result of an inability to change the flow of energy in yourself. This energy is stuck, unable to change from its current pattern. An increased awareness of your energy flow can reveal when energy is stuck and ways to unblock it. This will help to create a shift that must occur before energy can be realigned and controlled. You can move toward your ideal self only by first imagining it.

Each type of interaction carries with it particular energies; even memories carry certain vibrations with them. Energies of particular circumstances may stay the same or can change over time. Think back to how you felt about a particular childhood experience. For me, memories of learning new things carry with them happy and harmonious energies. My family and most of my teachers made learning fun and worthwhile, so this same energy carries through into adulthood and prompts me to be an enthusiastic lifelong learner. Some energies have definitely shifted over time, such as those associated with past close, personal relationships. I can see these circumstances and people from a different perspective, keeping the lessons and removing the emotion, thereby modifying the energies they hold and how they impact my life. The construct of energy can be applied to anything for a more objective, drama-free view of the world and your own life.

Using the methods discussed in this book, many of my clients and students have gotten off their sleep aids and antidepressant and anti-anxiety medications. There are maladies that certainly require these types of medications. However, the majority use them at the recommendation of a medical expert to dull and quiet the internal noise and soften the blow of the external energies bombarding them from the people and environments around them. Now they feel safe, in control, and are able to fully experience the world with clear energy and insight without the use of medication.

By consistently applying the dumping, grounding, and protection methods in this book, coupled with developing your energetic consciousness, it is possible to minimize anxiety and have a more positive outlook on life. It takes practice to stay energetically aware and to trust what you are sensing. There will be times when you slip back into old habits until you fully integrate the new way of looking at the world. Be patient with yourself. Apply the energy concepts you have learned to all circumstances and to yourself regularly, and you will create a shift in your perspective that opens the way to new possibilities for a happier, healthier life.

With blessings, Diane Wing.

Appendix A: Which Tools for Self-awareness Are Right for You?

Tools for Self-awareness Quiz—your personal style

Pick exactly five of the traits below that are most like you

1. I have a busy mind/have trouble getting mentally quiet
2. I trust information that comes seemingly out of the blue
3. I like to review the past and make sense of what happened
4. I like to keep a written log of experiences, feelings, and insights
5. I like to be in control
6. I tend to make decisions by going with gut feelings
7. I enjoy using multiple methods of gathering information
8. I like to discuss personal experiences with others
9. I tend to be visual
10. I believe in a higher self
11. I prefer getting information in an orderly format
12. I have creative outlets for self-expression

Quiz Scoring

Look at each of the five traits you picked and tally up the number of times each associated letter (A - D) appears altogether:

1. I have a busy mind/have trouble getting mentally quiet (A)
2. I trust information that comes seemingly out of the blue (D)
3. I like to review the past and make sense of what happened (B)
4. I like to keep a written log of experiences, feelings, and insights (C)
5. I like to be in control (A)
6. I tend to make decisions by going with gut feelings (D)
7. I enjoy using multiple methods of gathering information (B)
8. I like to discuss personal experiences with others (C)
9. I tend to be visual (A)
10. I believe in a higher self (D)
11. I prefer getting information in an orderly format (B)
12. I have creative outlets for self-expression (C)

Best tools based on your personal style:

Mostly *A*s: Active—Shamanic Journey, Guided Meditation—Takes you on a guided journey to discover aspects of yourself that lie hidden. Many times the imagery affords connection with animals or spirits that assist you in understanding the energies within you and around you.

Mostly *B*s: Intuitive—Tarot, Astrology, Runes, Numerology, Insight Stones®, Pathways—Cuts through the drama of a situation and enables you to tune in to what is important. Issues will surface regarding your personal and spiritual development. Much of what comes through is about your fears, hopes, and ambitions. Reveals underlying causes for what is being manifested in your life.

Mostly *C*s: Analytical—Assessments, Life Coaching—Provide insights into behaviors, personality, and tendencies in a variety of situations. Reveals your personal and communication styles. Helps to modify behaviors and gain objective insight.

Mostly *D*s: Expressive—Journaling, discussion with others—Allows uninhibited expression that acts as a release and a reveal into a person's true thoughts and feelings and how those impact that individual's behavior, choices, and life in general.

If you find that you score spans all four types, then you are able to successfully utilize multiple tools. Whichever you have the most of indicates a stronger affinity to that particular approach.

Appendix B: Group Work

Group energy is very powerful. It can either energize or diminish each member's individual vibrational level. Using the construct of energy in groups is a way to gain additional insights into your personal experiences, as well as to understand the energetic dynamics of the group itself.

Start by having everyone take the Wing Vibrational Quiz just before the gathering or during to get the most current vibrational level for each group member. See what the average level score is for the group as a whole and discuss the way that vibrational level affects how the group interacts with each other, as well as how the gathering itself raises or lowers the vibrational level of the group members. Do you find that your vibrational level rises or lowers when anticipating getting together with your group? What factors impact that shift? How can you work to keep the energy high within the group? Take the "temperature" of the group periodically to determine any energetic patterns that may be present.

Make it a practice to perform the dumping, grounding, and protection exercises at the beginning of the gathering. This will help to clear and strengthen the energy of individual group members and raise the overall group vibrational level.

The exercises in this book can be used as discussion points for the group gathering. Go through them in order or choose one at random. Each person could take a turn asking a question aloud and the group can discuss the exercise together and offer interpretations from their individual perspectives. With each contribution deeper understanding will emerge.

Exercises can be assigned prior to the gathering to give more time for discussion. Each person in the group can do the exercises on their own and then bring the results to compare with others. Individuals share their insights about their own results and then contribute thoughts about each others'. For example, "Exercise 2-2: Find Your Ideal Energizing Environment" would be completed by each group member. As a group, discuss what draws you to certain environments, the memories associated with those environments, and the effect it has on your mood when you are in it. See how many group members are attracted to similar environments. It could be a way to determine the best location when planning a group outing.

If your group is a book club, the Wing Vibrational Scale can be used as an enrichment activity. Each person measures the book itself on the Wing Vibrational Scale and then how the book made them feel personally using the Scale. Determine the vibrational level you experienced as you read the book, and then discuss why you felt that way. Then measure the emotional tone of the group that resulted from reading the book and assign it a group vibrational level rating. Did everyone feel similarly or were there significant variations among the members? See if there are vibrational patterns that are consistent when reading certain authors. Compare the vibrational level of the various books as an ongoing exercise. This will add depth to your discussions and allow for a new way to rate book club selections.

Using *The True Nature of Energy* for group work allows for additional insights and broader perspectives.

Glossary

Attunement – The act of opening one and bringing them into harmony with Universal Light Force to make it possible to channel energy. In Reiki, the student is attuned to particular symbols representative of energies used to heal and direct energy.

Aura/Auric Field –The personal energy field of an individual, which reflects the physical, emotional, mental, and spiritual condition of the person. The size of the auric field indicates the quantity and the color and texture the quality of that energy.

Chakra –Energy centers of the body. There are seven primary chakras. Starting with the seventh and working down to the first: the crown at the top of the head, third eye at the forehead between the eyes, throat, heart, solar plexus, sacral at the lower abdomen below the navel, and root at the base of the spine.

Clearing – Removing negative, heavy, or outmoded energies from the auric field. Doing so results in feeling lighter, having more mental clarity, more energy, and a brighter auric field.

The Chameleon Effect – Changing your behavior, appearance, or beliefs to conform to that of friends, colleagues, and family; changing to become who they wanted you to be or becoming whatever you need to be in order to cause the least amount of friction and the highest level of acceptance.

Endless Loop Complex – when people repeatedly complain about a particular relationship with their significant other, family member, or job.

Energy – The foundational component of energetic consciousness. Energy is everywhere, within and outside of you. The amount of energy you have indicates the quantity you have available to apply to your daily activities.

Ethereal (or Ethereal Presence) – An otherworldly being, entity, or presence that can be felt or sensed energetically, visually, or audibly, despite its immaterial nature.

Grounding – A means of attaching your energy to the Earth, allowing you to feel stable, balanced, and protected.

Higher Self – The metaphysical identity of the individual that transcends all physical realm constraints and limitations. It is that part of the self that connects with the Universal Energy, thereby making intuitive knowing possible.

Inner Magick – The magick within each person that includes intuitive abilities and unique gifts and talents. Tapping into and expressing Inner Magick allows the orchestration and creation of a life that is in accordance with the true self. Inner Magick allows a person to become more secure and more accepting of others.

Intuition – The inner guidance system everyone possesses that allows receipt of information unable to be known through common means.

Law of Return – Whatever type of energy you put out into the Universe will come back to you.

Phenomenological Truth – Everything you encounter and observe is subjected to your own perspective and filtered through your experience, thereby creating a personal version of what it means.

Reiki – A system of natural healing that channels energy from the Universe, into the practitioner, and out through the hands. Pronounced "ray-key", meaning Universal Life Force.

Selfless Devotion Syndrome – Being in a constant state of self-sacrifice to the point of losing oneself.

Source Energy – The Source goes by many names: God, Infinite Spirit, The One, The Source of All That Is, and Universal Energy, to name a few. Source Energy has no gender, no malice, no love, and no impetus of its own. It connects all beings and things together so that each impacts the other. The attitude of the energy is neutral, having no attachment to outcomes, nor directing activity.

Spiritual Unfoldment – A term used to describe the process of releasing old, outmoded behaviors, thoughts, and beliefs in order to come fully into the true self.

The Yeah, But... Consistency – The tendency of a constant complainer to resist most suggestions for change. Immediately following any suggestion, their response begins with "yeah, but." They tend to be closed overall and there is very little that can be done from the outside to intervene

Universal Energy – See "Source Energy"

Vibration – The frequency at which the personal auric field vibrates. The vibrational level indicates the quality of your energy.

Will – an inner strength that allows you to control your reactions, persist in the face of adversity, and set a goal or intention and achieve it. Will = Mind control + Self-discipline + Fortitude

About the Author

Diane Wing, M.A. is an author, teacher, personal transformation guide, and intuitive consultant. She has a Master's degree in clinical psychology and has been providing valuable insights for the highest good of her clients for over 27 years. Diane Wing is dedicated to helping empathic and energetically sensitive women get grounded and trust themselves, so they can live a peaceful and fulfilling life of joyful self-expression. She inspires others and teaches them to safely tap into the energies around them to turn anxiety into tranquility.

Diane is the author of several books, including *The True Nature of Tarot: Your Path to Personal Empowerment, Thorne Manor & Other Bizarre Tales*, a short story collection, and *Coven: The Scrolls of the Four Winds*, a novel.

She is the creator of two tools of self-empowerment "Insight Stones®: a game of self-awareness" and "Pathways - an interactive journey of self-discovery." She is the founder of Wing Academy of Unfoldment, a school of applied metaphysics.

Check out her on-demand radio show, Wing Academy Radio (dianewing.srbroadcasting.com), to discover ways to let go of what holds you back and apply spiritual concepts in everyday life.

Her website is DianeWing.com. You can also join her social network at www.DianeWing.tv.

Bibliography

Brennan, B. A. (1988). *Hands of light: A guide to healing through the human energy field : a new paradigm for the human being in health, relationship, and disease*. Toronto: Bantam Books.

Capra, F. (1975). *The Tao of physics: An exploration of the parallels between modern physics and eastern mysticism*. Berkeley: Shambhala.

Cunningham, S. (1988). *Cunningham's encyclopedia of crystal, gem & metal magic*. St. Paul, MN, U.S.A: Llewellyn Publications.

Denning, M., & Phillips, O. (2000). *The foundations of high magick*. Edison, NJ: Castle Books.

Emoto, M. (2004). *The hidden messages in water*. Hillsboro, Or: Beyond Words Pub.

Goswami, A., Reed, R. E., & Goswami, M. (1993). *The self-aware universe: How consciousness creates the material world*. New York: Putnam's Sons.

Herbert, N. (1985). *Quantum reality: Beyond the new physics*. Garden City, N.Y: Anchor Press/Doubleday.

Hopman, E. E. (1991). *Tree medicine, tree magic*. Custer, Wash: Phoenix Pub.

McTaggart, L. (2003). *The Field: The quest for the secret force of the universe*. New York, NY: HarperCollins Publishers: Quill.

Melody. (1995). *Love is in the earth: A kaleidoscope of crystals: update : the reference book describing the metaphysical properties of the mineral kingdom*. Wheat Ridge, CO: Earth-Love Pub. House.

Neville, . (1992). *The power of awareness*. Marina del Rey, CA: DeVorss Publications.

Paterson, J. M. (1996). *Tree wisdom*. London: Thorsons.

Simmons, R., Ahsian, N., & Raven, H. (2007). *The book of stones: Who they are & what they teach*. East Montpelier, VT: Heaven and Earth Pub.

Sui, C. K. (1990). *Pranic healing.* York Beach, Me: S. Weiser.

Walker, E. H. (2000). *The physics of consciousness: The quantum minds and the meaning of life.* Cambridge, Mass: Perseus Books.

Wing, D. (2010). *The true nature of tarot: Your path to personal empowerment.* Ann Arbor, MI: Marvelous Spirit Press.

Index

Get Better Results by Increasing Your Psychic Sensitivity!

The True Nature of Tarot dispels the myths and negative connotations that surround the tarot by sharing the personal experiences of the author, Diane Wing, a tarot reader with 25 years of experience.

Tarot is discussed as a tool of enlightenment and understanding. Diane Wing shares intuitive techniques for reading that take you beyond the conventional card meanings and deep into tarot as a tool to channel energy and increase psychic sensitivity:

- Develop your own style of reading tarot, from choosing your deck to pulling information from the cards.
- Learn how a reading is experienced from the perspectives of both the reader and the inquirer.
- Understand the variables that impact the accuracy of your reading.
- Discover ways to increase the amount of information pulled from the tarot.
- Become expert at grounding and centering to maximize your energetic stability on a daily basis.
- Learn powerful spreads that give you ways to see interactions between the cards.
- Increase your awareness of the ethics of imparting information.

ISBN 978-1-61599-021-4 • Paperback $19.95
Also available in hardcover and eBook formats
Learn More at www.ForestWitch.com

From Marvelous Spirit Press
www.MarvelousSpirit.com

CPSIA information can be obtained at www.ICGtesting.com
Printed in the USA
BVOW000243090713

325226BV00005B/11/P